ESSENTIALS OF FINGERPRINT EXAMINATION

A LABORATORY GUIDE

DR. RAJU NANDHAKUMAR &
MS. LABHINI RAHANGDALE

INDIA • SINGAPORE • MALAYSIA

CONTENTS

PREFACE

In the intricate tapestry of human identity, fingerprints are the threads that weave together the unique narrative of each individual. Like a masterful work of art, fingerprints are a distinctive blend of patterns, shapes, and lines that defy replication. For forensic scientists, fingerprint examination is an art and a science that requires precision, patience, and dedication. It is a painstaking process that demands attention to detail, a keen eye for observation, and a deep understanding of the intricacies of friction ridges. In this laboratory guide, we invite you to enter the fascinating world of fingerprint examination, where the minutiae of detail holds the key to unlocking the secrets of identity, truth, and justice. Within these pages, we will delve into the essentials of fingerprint examination, from the fundamental principles of friction ridge analysis to the advanced techniques and comparison. This book is designed to serve as a comprehensive resource for forensic professionals, students, and anyone seeking to master the art and science of fingerprint examination. Through a combination of theoretical foundations, practical protocols, and real-world examples, we aim to equip you with the knowledge, skills, and confidence to navigate the complexities of fingerprint analysis with precision and accuracy. As you embark on this journey into the world of fingerprint examination, remember that every print tells a story, every detail holds a secret, and every comparison has the power to reveal the truth. Let us unravel the mysteries of the fingerprint together and may the unique patterns and shapes that we encounter inspire us to seek justice, uphold the truth, and honor the individuality that makes us human. The purpose of this lab manual is to bridge the gap between theoretical knowledge and practical application. It is designed for students, forensic professionals, and enthusiasts who seek to understand and master the art of fingerprint analysis. The manual covers a broad spectrum of topics, from the basic anatomy of fingerprints to advanced techniques in fingerprint identification and comparison. This fingerprint laboratory manual contains a series of experiments that provide practical insight into fingerprint examination. Fingerprint evidence is crucial in court proceedings, making it essential for forensic enthusiasts to have a thorough understanding of efficient, practical techniques for fingerprint analysis. This manual offers comprehensive assistance for conducting fingerprint examinations. We extend our gratitude to the many forensic experts, educators, and practitioners who have contributed to the development of this manual. Their insights and experiences have been invaluable in creating a resource that is both informative and practical. Whether you are a novice starting your forensic journey or a seasoned professional seeking to refine your skills, this manual serves as a trusted companion in your exploration.

FROM THE AUTHORS

Fingerprint analysis stands as one of the oldest and most reliable methods in the field of forensic science. Since its initial use in the late 19th century, fingerprint analysis has evolved from a rudimentary practice into a sophisticated science integral to modern criminal investigations. This manual aims to provide a comprehensive guide to the principles, techniques, and applications of fingerprint analysis in forensic investigations. Fingerprint evidence is a cornerstone of forensic science due to its uniqueness and permanence. Each individual's fingerprints are distinct, providing a reliable means of identification that remains consistent over a lifetime. This type of evidence is critical in criminal investigations, as it can link a suspect to a crime scene or verify identities. Fingerprint analysis involves comparing the minutiae patterns found in the ridges and valleys of fingerprints to known prints, aiding in the accurate identification of individuals. Its ability to provide irrefutable proof makes fingerprint evidence invaluable in solving crimes, securing convictions, and ensuring justice is served.

This manual has been meticulously crafted for the Forensic Dermatoglyphics Laboratory, focusing on experiments that complement the theoretical concepts of Forensic Science. The primary objective of this laboratory is to cultivate students' understanding of crime scene investigation principles and fundamental analysis techniques. Additionally, it aims to equip students with the necessary laboratory skills to conduct accurate and precise evidence analysis. It is imperative that students demonstrate proficiency in the theoretical foundations of crime scene investigation procedures and apply this knowledge to manage and interpret fingerprint evidence effectively. Through this laboratory experience, students will gain a comprehensive appreciation for the complexities of forensic analysis and develop the competence needed to excel in this field.

Format of the Lab Report:

You should prepare your lab reports by hand. They should include tables and illustrations where necessary. Typically, a lab report should contain the following sections: title page, introduction, experimental section, results and discussion, conclusion, and references. Your title page should be a separate page, including the title of the project, which might simply be the name of the experiment, your name, the name of the course, and the date the report is due.

- **Safety Rules:** The laboratory is not a dangerous place to work as long as all necessary precautions are taken seriously. In the following paragraphs, those important precautions are described. Everyone who works and performs experiments in a laboratory must follow these safety rules at all times. Students who do not obey the safety rules will not be allowed to enter and do any type of work in the laboratory, and they will be counted as absent. It is the student's responsibility to read all the safety rules carefully before the first lab meeting.
- **Gloves and Headgear**: Crime scene Investigation process includes analysis of samples and many rigorous activities. It is important to wear gloves/ Lab Coat and Head Gear etc.
- **Food and Smoking:** Eating and drinking any type of food are always prohibited in the laboratory. Smoking is not allowed. Anyone who refuses to do so will be forced to leave the laboratory.
- **Clothing and Footwear**: Everyone must wear a lab coat during the lab, and no shorts or sandals are allowed. Long hair should be securely tied back to avoid the risk of setting it on fire. If large amounts of chemicals are spilled on your body, immediately remove the contaminated clothing and use the safety shower if available. Make sure to inform your instructor about the problem. Do not leave your coats and backpacks on the bench. No personnel gadgets are allowed in the lab.
- **Fire:** In case of fire or an accident, inform your instructor at once. Note the location of fire extinguishers and, if available, safety showers and safety blankets as soon as you enter the laboratory so that you may use them if needed. Never perform an unauthorised experiment in the laboratory. Never assume that it is not necessary to inform

your instructor of small accidents. Notify him/her no matter how slight it is.

- **Laboratory Care and Waste Disposal:** Remember that the equipment you use in this laboratory will be used by many other students. Please leave the equipment and all workspaces as you wish to find them. After the end of each lab, clean off your work area. Wash your glassware. When weighing any material on the balance, do not weigh directly onto the balance pan. Weigh your material on a piece of weighing paper. The balances are very sensitive instruments and should be treated with great care.
- **Waste Disposal**: If you take more reagents than you need, do not put excess back into the bottle. It may be contaminated. Treat it as waste and dispose of it accordingly. It is most likely that, during any experiment, you will perform, you will generate some waste chemicals and solutions to dispose of. Never put them down the sink unless your instructor specifically tells them to do so. There will be inorganic, organic, and solid waste containers in the lab. Dispose of your waste in the appropriate container.

This manual provides a comprehensive overview of the necessary procedures and protocols for running a forensic Dermatoglyphics laboratory. Adhering to these guidelines is crucial in maintaining the accuracy and credibility of fingerprint evidence, which is essential in aiding criminal investigations and legal proceedings.

1

TO RECORD PLAIN AND ROLLED FINGERPRINT IMPRESSION

AIM

To record the Plain and Rolled Fingerprint Impression of the given forensic samples.

MATERIALS REQUIRED

Recording the performa of fingerprint, pencil, scale, glass slab, ink, and roller.

THEORY

Fingerprints are unique patterns formed by the ridges on the skin of human fingers and palms. They are widely used in forensic science for identification purposes due to their distinctiveness and permanence throughout an individual's life. Collecting fingerprints from suspects is a critical aspect of criminal investigations, and one common method used for this purpose is the ink and roller technique.

The ink and roller technique, also known as the inked impression method, is a traditional but effective way of capturing fingerprints. Here is how the process typically unfolds:

1. **Preparation**: Before collecting fingerprints, law enforcement officers ensure that the suspect's hands are clean and dry. This helps to obtain clear and legible prints without any smudges or distortions.

2. **Ink Application**: The officer applies a thin layer of fingerprint ink onto a glass or metal plate using a roller. The ink should have a smooth consistency to ensure even coverage and to prevent excess ink from smudging the print.
3. **Rolling the Finger**: The suspect is instructed to roll their fingertip from one side to the other on the inked plate. The rolling action ensures that the entire fingerprint pattern is transferred onto the finger evenly.
4. **Transfer to paper**: Once the fingerprint is inked onto the suspect's finger, the officer guides the suspect to roll their finger onto a clean, white fingerprint card or paper. The paper used is typically thick and has a smooth surface to capture the details of the fingerprint clearly.
5. **Repeating the Process**: If necessary, the process is repeated for each finger on both hands to collect a complete set of fingerprints. This ensures that all potential points of comparison are available for forensic analysis.
6. **Recording Details**: Alongside each fingerprint impression, the officer records relevant information such as the suspect's name, date, time, and the finger from which the print was taken. This documentation is crucial for maintaining an accurate chain of custody and providing context to the collected evidence.
7. **Cleaning Up**: After obtaining the fingerprints, any excess ink on the suspect's fingers is carefully wiped off using a clean cloth or tissue. Additionally, the inked plate and roller are cleaned to prevent contamination and ensure that they are ready for future use.

The ink and roller technique is considered a reliable method for collecting fingerprints, especially in situations where electronic fingerprint scanners may not be readily available or suitable. However, precision and careful handling are required to avoid smudging or distorting the prints, which could compromise their accuracy as forensic evidence.

Once collected, the fingerprints are analyzed and compared to known prints from crime scenes or databases to determine if there is a match, thus aiding in the identification of suspects and contributing to the resolution of criminal cases.

PROCEDURE

- **Preparation**: Before collecting fingerprints, students ensured that the suspect's/subject hands were clean and dry. This helps to obtain clear and legible prints without any smudges or distortions.
- **Ink Application**: The student applied a thin layer of fingerprint ink onto a glass or metal plate using a roller. The ink should have a smooth consistency to ensure even coverage and to prevent excess ink from smudging the print.
- **Rolling the Finger**: The suspect/subject is instructed to roll their fingertip from one side to the other on the inked plate. The rolling action ensures that the entire fingerprint pattern is transferred onto the finger evenly.
- **Transfer to paper**: Once the fingerprint is inked onto the suspect's/ subject finger, the officer guides the suspect to roll their finger onto a clean, white fingerprint card or paper. The paper used is typically thick and has a smooth surface to capture the details of the fingerprint clearly.

ROLLING INKED PRINTS

- Roll the finger on the ink so the entire pad is covered nail to nail
- Thumb is rolled towards the subject's body (1st Digit rolled)
- Fingers are rolled away from the subject's body (Order - Index, Middle, Ring, Little finger)
- Plain Impressions done last (4 fingers 1st, then thumbs)

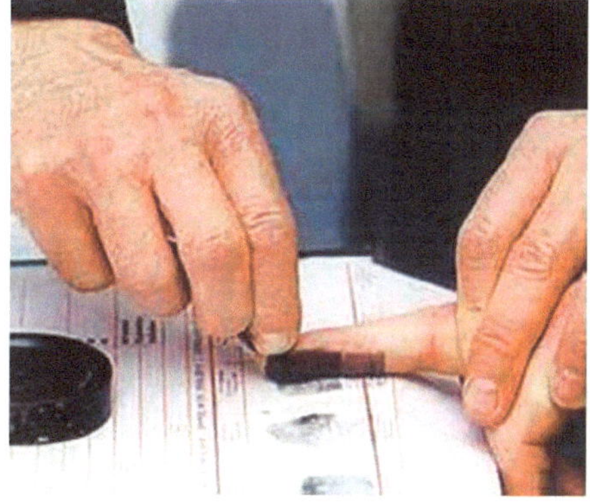

OBSERVATION

Paste the fingerprint A4 sheet where you have collected/recorded all ten fingers in the rolled and plain way of recording fingers on the day of lab. Paste it on the blank side of your fair record.

CONCLUSION

We have successfully studied how to record/collect fingerprints from an individual using ink and roller.

FORENSIC SIGNIFICANCE

One of the key factors that make fingerprints valuable in forensic science is their uniqueness. No two individuals, including identical twins, have the same fingerprints. This uniqueness allows forensic experts to identify or eliminate suspects from a crime scene.

VIVA QUESTIONS

1. Define Fingerprint.
2. How to record rolled impression from a suspect.
3. Define different patterns of Fingerprints.
4. How are fingerprints forensically important?
5. What are the different patterns of Fingerprints?
6. How are fingerprints classified?
7. Differentiate between Plain, Whorl, and central pocket loops.
8. What is a double loop/twin loop?
9. List out the principles followed by fingerprints.
10. Expand AFIS.

11. Define Dactyloscopy?
12. What is the need to record plain and rolled fingerprints separately?
13. What are ridges and furrows in Fingerprints?
14. How are radical and ulnar loops different from each other?
15. Mention any three unique properties of fingerprinting to identify the suspects.

CASE STUDIES

2

IDENTIFYING FINGERPRINT PATTERN

AIM

To identify Fingerprint Patterns by examination of different fingerprint samples.

THEORY

A fingerprint **impression is made by the papillary ridges on the ends of the fingers and thumbs**. Fingerprints afford an infallible means of personal identification because the ridge arrangement on every finger of every human being is unique and does not alter with growth or age.

There are several variants of the Henry system, but that used by the Federal Bureau of Investigation (FBI) in the United States recognises eight different types of patterns: **radial loop, ulnar loop, double loop, central pocket loop, plain arch, tented arch, plain whorl, and accidental**.

There are three major types of Fingerprints:

The 3 Major Types of Fingerprints

No 2: The Whorl

No. 1: The Arch

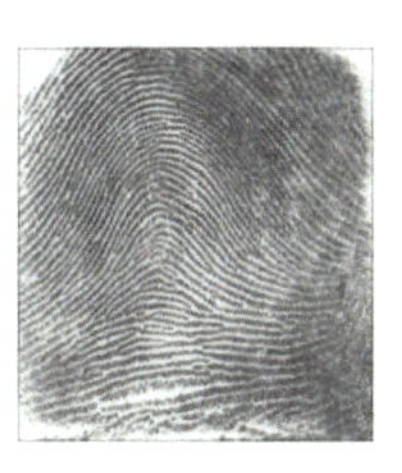

No. 3: The Loop

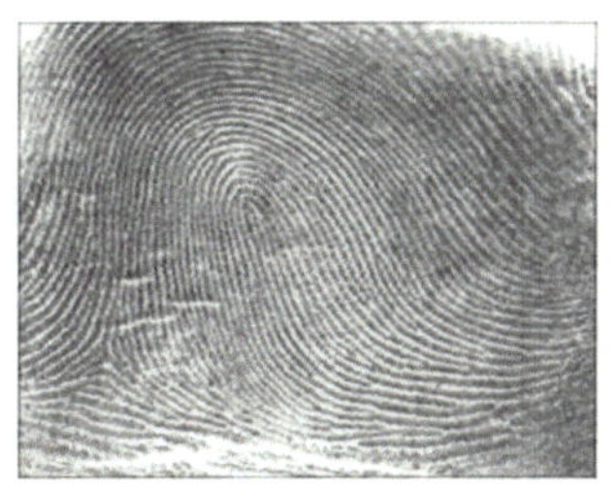

1. The ARCH

This is the rarest type of fingerprint. In fact, about **5% of the world's population** has this fingerprint pattern. Its lack of cores, lines, or deltas makes it unique. Within this pattern, two other sub-categories emerge:

- **Plain Arch** – Raised ridges characterise this pattern and they extend from one side of the finger to the other in a continuous fashion. This pattern makes up a mere 5% of the total population, making it the rarest type.
- **Tented Arch** – Similar to the plain arch, the tented arch also has raised ridges flowing in the same fashion. The distinct difference comes in the pitch of the raised ridge. The tented arch has a sharper edge compared to the plain arch, which forms a tent-like shape.

2. THE WHORL

This fingerprint pattern makes up about **25 to 35 percent of the total population**. Unlike the arch pattern, whorls have a core and two deltas. It's only similar to the arch in the sub-categories; it has two:

- **Plain Whorl** –A plain whorl will make a circular pattern that represents a swirl or a spiral. This circular pattern is unbroken, and this revolution that forms at the center is a result of at least a single ridge.

3. THE LOOP

This is the most popular fingerprint pattern. Indeed, **60 to 70 percent of the total population has** this pattern. In the loop pattern, there must be at least a single core and delta.

Unlike the rest of the patterns, the loop has three sub-categories:

- **Ulnar Loop** –In this pattern, the ridges turn backward, but they don't make a full turn. To identify an ulnar loop, you'll notice the loops moving toward the small finger. You'll see these turns only if you view them on the hand and not on a card.
- **Radial Loop** –This pattern is similar to the ulnar loop, but the difference is the turns point toward the thumb instead of the small finger.

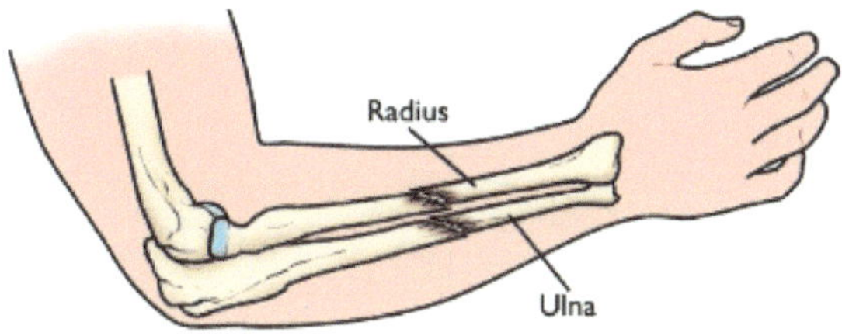

4. COMPOSITE PATTERNS

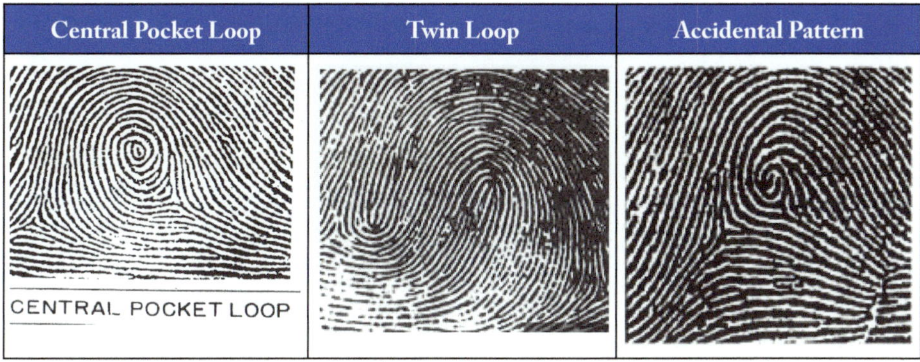

Central Pocket Loop	Twin Loop	Accidental Pattern
CENTRAL POCKET LOOP		

1. Central Pocket Loop

A type of print pattern that has two deltas and at least one friction ridge that makes one complete circuit, which may be spiral, oval, circular, or any variant of a circle; an imaginary line drawn between the two deltas does not touch or cross the "central pocket."

2. Twin or Double Loop

A type of print pattern that consists of two separate loop formations with two separate and distinct sets of shoulders and two deltas.

3. Accidental Pattern

Any pattern which doesn't match with other types listed here fall in this category. These patterns contain two features of the tented arch, loop or whorl patterns.

Accidental whorls can follow in some of the arrangements given below:

1. Loop and a whorl
2. Loop and a tented arch
3. Loop and central pocket loop
4. Double loop and central pocket loop

REQUIREMENTS

A4 size sheets, magnifying glass, scale, pencil, ink pad, and fingerprint impression samples.

PROCEDURE

PART A

Sample Preparation for Examination

- Take fingerprint impressions on A4 sheets from all the subjects.
- The collection of fingerprint impressions was done using an ink pad.
- Press your finger on the ink pad with a proper amount of pressure and then give your impression on A4 sheets.
- After sample preparation/collection, we examined the samples.

PART B

Identification of Fingerprint Patterns based on analysis of samples

- We examined impressions using a magnifying glass.
- Observed all the features of fingerprints, including flow and direction of ridges.
- We also observed the presence or absence of core and delta in finger impressions.
- We also observed a number of deltas to identify patterns.
- After analyzing all these things, we distinguished all the finger impressions in the category of a particular pattern.

OBSERVATION

Sr. No	Finger Print Impression Samples	Name of Pattern	Description/ Reason
1.			
2.			
3.			

RESULT

Different fingerprint patterns have been successfully identified and studied.

VIVA QUESTIONS

1. What are the three main types of fingerprint patterns?
2. How is a "loop" pattern identified in a fingerprint?
3. What is the difference between a "radial" and "ulnar" loop?
4. How is a "whorl" pattern identified in a fingerprint?
5. What is the difference between a "plain arch" and a "tented arch"?
6. How many types of whorls are there in fingerprint analysis?
7. What is a "central pocket loop" in fingerprint analysis?
8. How is a "lateral pocket loop" different from a "central pocket loop"?
9. What is a "twinned loop" in fingerprint analysis?

10. How is a "plain arch" different from a "tented arch"?
11. What is the "core" of a fingerprint pattern?
12. How do you determine the "delta" point in a fingerprint pattern?
13. What is the significance of the "ridge count" in fingerprint analysis?
14. How do you distinguish between a "loop" and a "whorl" pattern?
15. What is the importance of identifying fingerprint patterns in forensic science?

CASE STUDIES

3

ANALYSIS TO CARRY OUT RIDGE CHARACTERISTICS IN FINGERPRINT

AIM

To record fingerprints of neighbours, and your home using ink, grease, blood, etc., and study the type of fingerprint and ridge characteristics.

THEORY

Fingerprints are unique patterns made by friction ridges (raised) and furrows (recessed). No two people have the same fingerprints. Even identical twins with identical DNA have different fingerprints. This uniqueness allows fingerprints to be used in all sorts of ways, including biometric security in criminal situations, etc. Fingerprint analysis has been used to identify suspects and solve crimes for more than 100 years, and it remains an extremely valuable tool for law enforcement. Also, a person's fingerprints remain essentially unchanged throughout their lifetime. There are three types of fingerprints: 1. Patent fingerprint 2. Latent fingerprint, and 3. Impressed fingerprint. Patent fingerprints are made by a liquid or powder that sticks to the finger and then transfers to a surface, leaving an easily visible fingerprint behind. Substances that can leave patent fingerprints are ink, blood, dirt, flour, grease, etc. A latent print is an impression of the friction skin of the fingers or palms of the hands that has been transferred to another surface. A latent fingerprint is often analyzed in the crime. Impressed fingers are those that have been made of soft material or tissue by pressing down with the finger or hand.

Patterns of fingerprint: Friction ridge patterns are grouped into three distinct types—loops, whorls, and arches—each with unique variations, depending on the shape and relationship of the ridges:

1. **Loops** - prints that recurve back on themselves to form a loop shape. Divided into radial loops (pointing toward the radius bone or thumb) and ulnar loops (pointing toward the ulna bone or little finger). These are named after the radial bone and ulnar bone in the hand. Loops account for approximately 60 percent of pattern types.
2. **Arches** - create a wave-like pattern and include plain arches and tented arches. Tented arches rise to a sharper point than plain arches. Arches make up about five percent of all pattern types.
3. **Whorls** - form circular or spiral patterns, like tiny whirlpools. There are four groups of whorls: Further there are several types as shown in the figure. Whorls make up about 35 percent of pattern types.

Fingerprint is the impression made by the papillary ridges on the ends of the fingers and thumbs. Fingerprints afford an infallible means of personal identification because the ridge arrangement on every finger of every human being is unique and does not alter with growth or age. There are several variants of the Henry system, but that used by the Federal Bureau of Investigation (FBI) in the United States recognises eight different types of patterns: radial loop, ulnar loop, double loop, central pocket loop, plain arch, tented arch, plain whorl, and accidental. The uniqueness of a fingerprint is exclusively determined by the local ridge characteristics and their relationships. The ridges and valleys in a fingerprint alternate, flowing in a local constant direction.

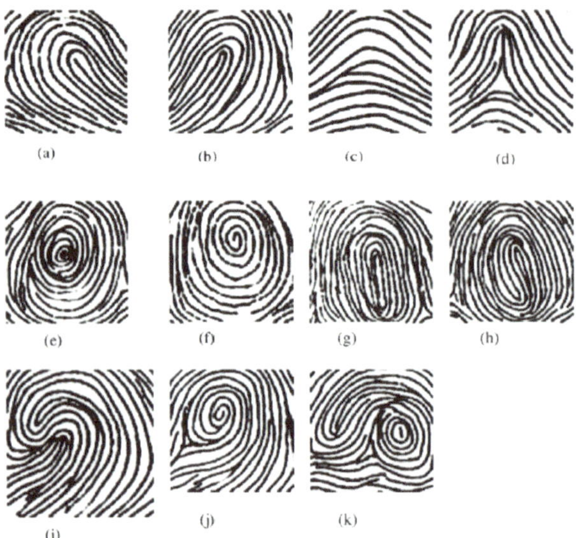

Basic patterns of fingerprints-(a) Ulnar Loop (b) Radial Loop (c) Simple Arch (d) Tented Arch (e) Concentric Whorl (f) Spiral Whorl pattern (g) Press Whorl (h) Imploding Whorl (i) Composite Whorl (j) Peacock's Eye (k) Variant pattern

RIDGE CHARACTERISTICS/MINUTIEA

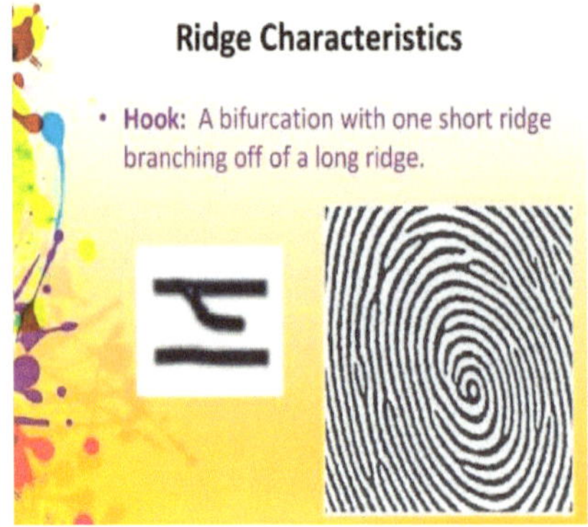

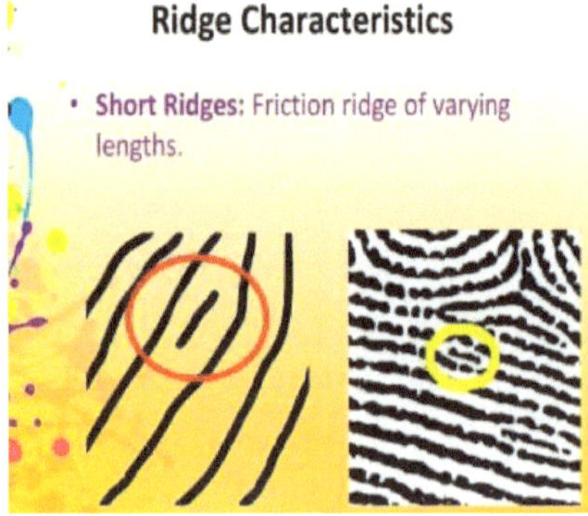

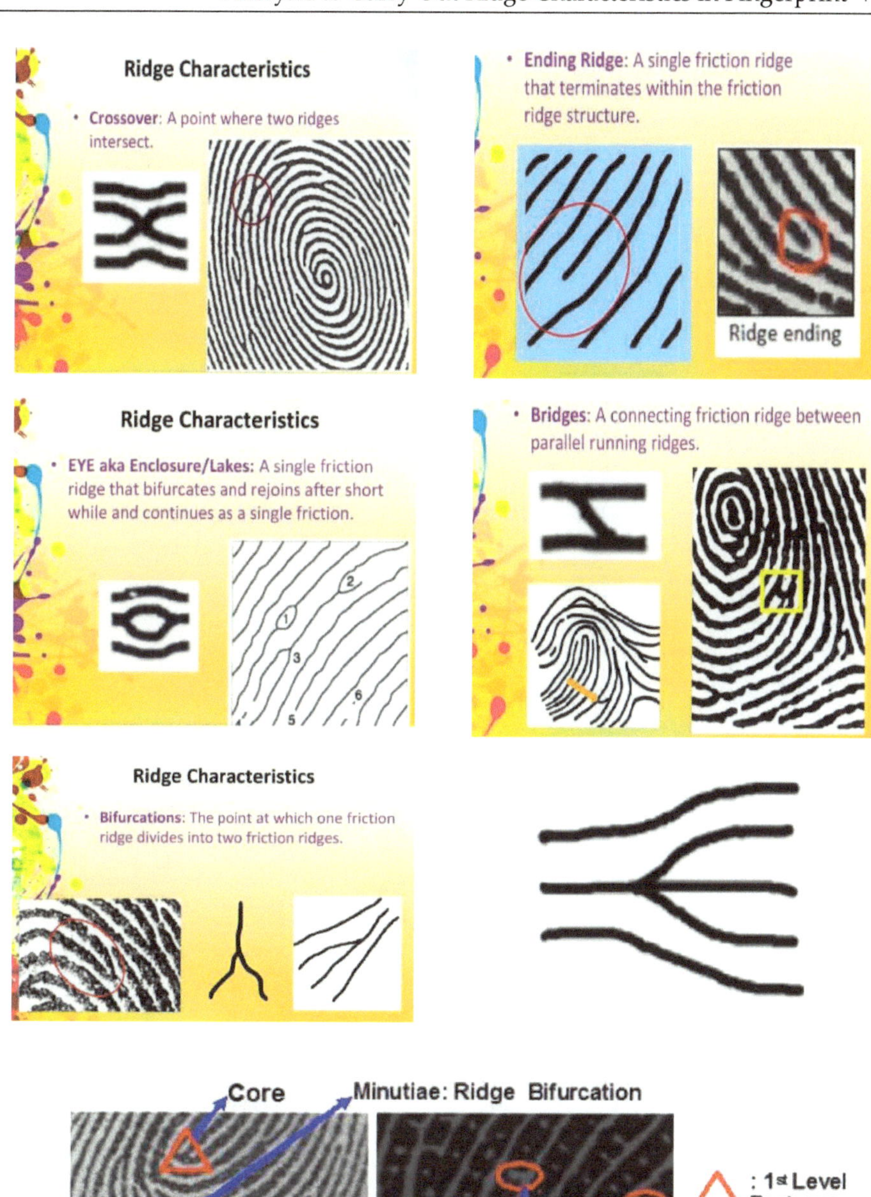

Other Ridge Characteristics

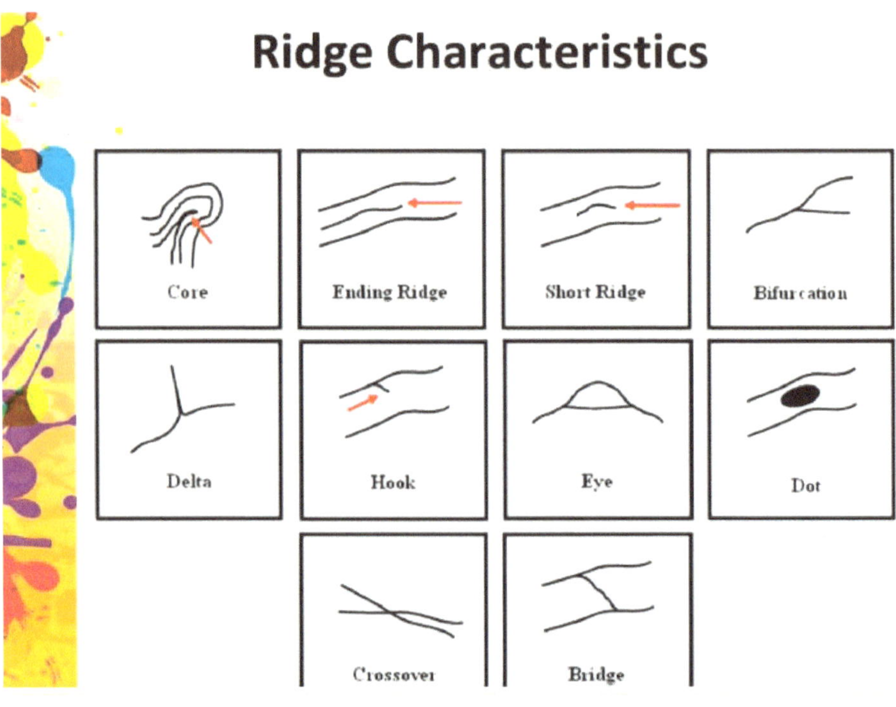
Ridge Characteristics
Core
Ending Ridge
Short Ridge
Bifurcation
Delta
Hook
Eye
Dot
Crossover
Bridge

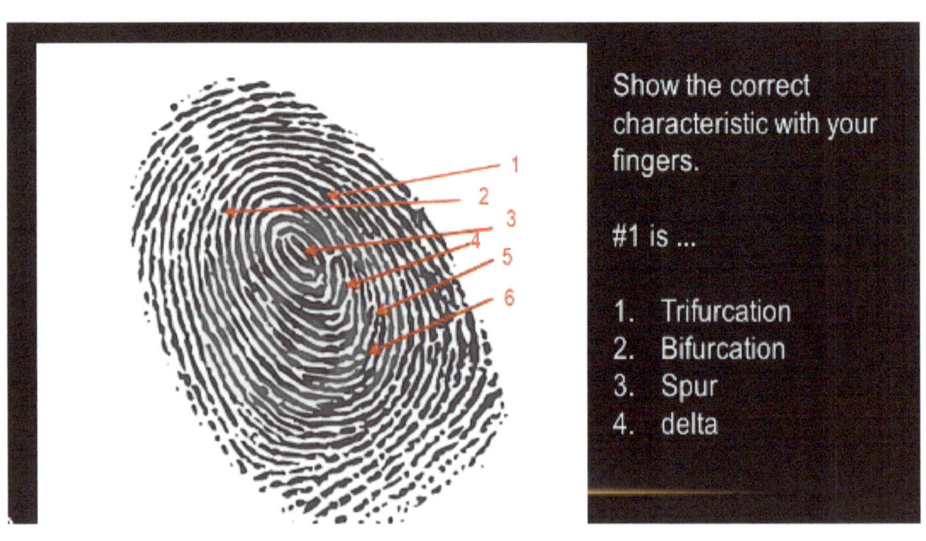
1
2
3
4
5
6
Show the correct characteristic with your fingers.
#1 is ...
1. Trifurcation
2. Bifurcation
3. Spur
4. delta

REQUIREMENTS

A4 size sheets, magnifying glass, scale, pencil, ink pad, and fingerprint impression samples.

PROCEDURE

PART A

Sample Preparation for Examination

- Take fingerprint impressions on A4 sheets from all the subjects.
- The collection of fingerprint impressions was done using an ink pad.
- Press your finger on the ink pad with a proper amount of pressure and then give your impression on A4 sheets.
- After sample preparation/collection, we examined the samples.

PART B

Identification of Fingerprint Minutiae based on analysis of samples

- We examined impressions using a magnifying glass.
- Observed all the features of fingerprints, including flow and direction of ridges.
- We also observed the presence or absence of core and delta in finger impressions.
- We then determined patterns of fingerprints.
- We then observed ridge characteristics in each finger impression.

OBSERVATION

Sr. No	FINGER PRINT IMPRESSION SAMPLES	NAME OF PATTERN	MINUTIAE
1.		Arch, Whorl, Loop?	1) Bifurcation 2)Enclosure etc.
2.			
3.			
4.			
5.			

RESULTS

Identification of ridge characteristics has been successfully studied.

FORENSIC SIGNIFICANCE

One of the basic importance of fingerprints is that it helps in establishing identity of a person with minimum time and efforts; and then enabling speedy investigation. The fingerprint evidence has been referred to as reliable piece of evidence. They are also permanent and do not undergo any change.

VIVA QUESTIONS

1. What is the persistence of fingerprints?
2. The most common type of fingerprint is ———
3. What materials can be used to get a patent fingerprint?
4. What are the types of fingerprint patterns?
5. What are the subtypes of loop patterns?
6. Differentiate between patent and latent fingerprints.
7. Is it possible to get a fingerprint from the coarse surface? Justify your answer
8. Expand NCRB. Where is it located?
9. Name any two software/programs to compare the fingerprints.
10. Name any five ridge characteristics.
11. Define fingerprints.
12. Define Loop, arch, and whorl patterns.
13. In which fingerprint pattern are the core and delta absent?
14. What is a twin loop pattern?
15. What is a minutia?
16. Define hook and bifurcation.
17. Define island.

CASE STUDIES

4

TO PERFORM RIDGE COUNTING IN LOOP PATTERN

AIM

To perform the Ridge Counting in Loop Pattern.

THEORY

Ridge counting is a crucial aspect of fingerprint analysis, particularly in loop patterns. It helps forensic experts identify and classify fingerprints accurately, aiding in criminal investigations and identification processes. This lab manual provides a step-by-step guide to conducting ridge counting in loop pattern analysis.

MATERIALS REQUIRED

1. Fingerprint samples (actual or printed copies)
2. Magnifying glass or microscope
3. Ridge counter tool or ruler
4. Pen and paper for recording data

PROCEDURE

Preparation of Fingerprint Samples

- Obtain fingerprint samples either from a database or by taking fresh prints using fingerprint ink and paper.
- Ensure that the fingerprint samples are clear and distinct, free from smudges or distortions.

Identification of Loop Patterns

- Examine the fingerprint samples under a magnifying glass or microscope to identify loop patterns.
- Loop patterns are characterised by a series of ridges entering from one side, curving, and exiting from the same side.

Selection of Reference Point

- **Choose a reference point within the loop pattern where ridge counting will begin.**
- **Typically, the reference point is where the ridge pattern starts to curve inward.**

Ridge Counting

- Using a ridge counter tool or a ruler, start counting the ridges from the reference point.
- Count each ridge that crosses the imaginary line drawn from the reference point towards the center of the loop.
- Continue counting until reaching a predetermined reference point on the opposite side of the loop.
- Ridges, including in ridge counting and their numerical values –
  1. An inland ridge or dot is assigned a ridge count of 1.
  2. A short ridge is also assigned a ridge count of 1.
  3. A long ridge is likewise assigned a ridge count of 1.

4. An abrupt ending ridge is assigned a ridge count of 1.
5. If a ridge bifurcates into two across the imaginary line, it is assigned a ridge count of 2.
6. If the point of origin of a bifurcating ridge is on the line of count, it is assigned a ridge count of 2.
7. If the legs of the enclosure or eyelet ridge are on the line of the count, it is assigned a ridge count of 2.
8. If the intersection of two enclosures is on the line of count, it is assigned a ridge count of 4.

These guidelines serve as a standardised approach to accurately determine the ridge count in different ridge patterns.

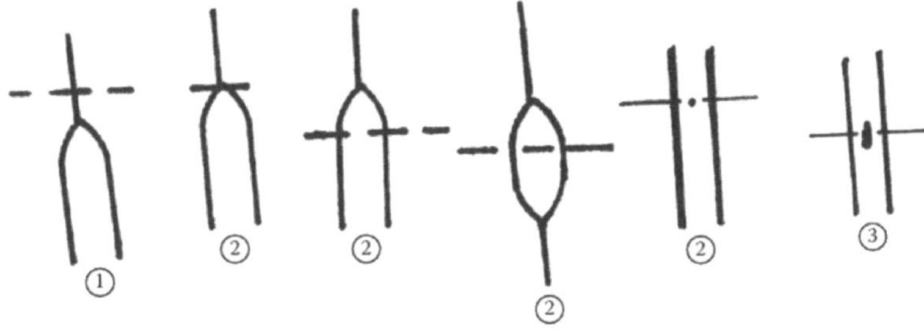

Recording Data

- Record the total number of ridges counted for each loop pattern.
- Note down any distinguishing features or characteristics observed during the ridge counting process.

Repeat for Accuracy

- Repeat the ridge counting process multiple times to ensure accuracy and consistency.
- If there are discrepancies in the counts, reconcile them by taking an average or by further examination.

Analysis and Interpretation

- Compare the ridge counts obtained from different loop patterns.
- Use the ridge counts along with other features of the fingerprints to make classifications and identifications.
- Document findings and interpretations thoroughly for future reference.

OBSERVATION

Sr. No	LOOP PATTERN	NUMBER OF RIDGE COUNT
1.	Paste the image of loop impression 	Ridge count no: 6, 8, 7, and 15 etc.????
2.		

CONCLUSION

Ridge counting has been successfully done.

FORENSIC SIGNIFICANCE

Ridge counting in loop pattern analysis is a fundamental skill in forensic science. By following the prescribed procedures outlined in this manual, forensic experts can accurately count ridges and utilise this information in fingerprint identification and classification processes.

VIVA QUESTIONS

1. What is the primary purpose of ridge counting in fingerprint analysis?
2. Which type of fingerprint pattern features a circular or oval shape?
3. What is the core of a loop pattern in fingerprint analysis?
4. How many ridges are typically found between the core and delta points in a loop pattern?
5. What is the purpose of identifying the delta point in ridge counting?
6. In which direction do the ridges flow in a radial loop pattern?
7. What is the name of the point where the ridges meet in a loop pattern?
8. How many types of loop patterns are there in fingerprint analysis?
9. Which loop pattern has ridges that enter from one side and exit from the other?
10. What is the term for the count of ridges between the core and delta points in a fingerprint?

CASE STUDIES

5

PERFORM RIDGE TRACING IN GIVEN FINGERPRINT SAMPLES

AIM

To perform ridge tracing in given fingerprint samples.

THEORY

Ridge tracing refers to the process of following and delineating the path of the ridges within a fingerprint.

Purpose and Significance

Ridge tracing helps in visualizing and understanding the ridge patterns present in a fingerprint. It aids in identifying various types of ridge patterns, such as loops, whorls, and arches, which are crucial for fingerprint classification. Ridge tracing facilitates the identification and comparison of fingerprints, especially when analyzing latent prints obtained from crime scenes.

MATERIALS REQUIRED

A4 sheet, Pencil, scale, Fingerprint ink and roller, Ink slab, etc.

PROCEDURE

1. Ridge tracing is performed using specialised tools such as magnifying lenses, microscopes, etc.
2. The process involves carefully following the ridges from their starting point (core or delta) to the endpoint, considering their flow, shape, and continuity.
3. Tracing the ridges includes recording the overall pattern and noting any deviations, bifurcations, or ridge characteristics along the way.

Methodology

1. Establish deltas.
2. Starting at the left delta, trace ridges, moving outward away from the center of the pattern to where the ridge ends. Continue tracing until the point nearest or opposite the extreme right delta is reached.
3. If the ridge bifurcates, the lower branch is followed.
4. Examine other apparent ridge endings in the pattern to ensure that the ridge actually ends and is not caused by other factors such as improper inking, the presence of debris, and the like.
5. The number of ridges between the tracing ridge and the right delta is counted.

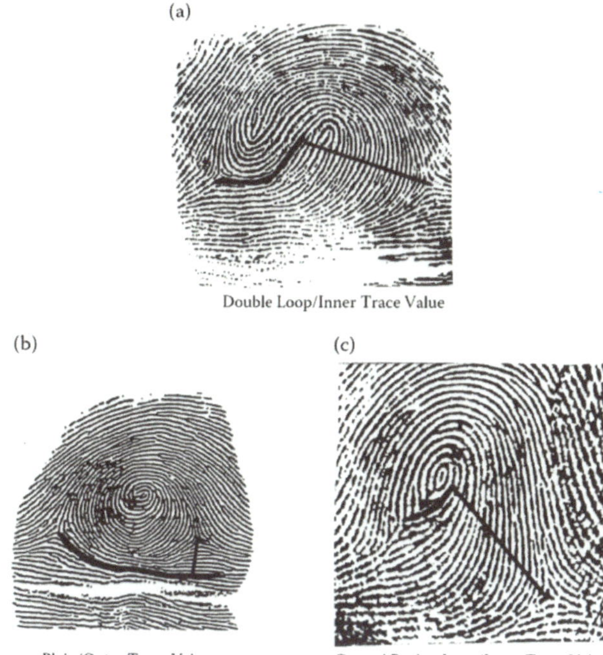

Double Loop/Inner Trace Value

Plain/Outer Trace Value

Central Pocket Loop/Inner Trace Value

Values:

- **Inner (I):** If the traced ridge goes above or reverse back inner before reaching the right delta, and there are three or more interviewing ridges between the traced ridge and the right delta. It is considered as **INNER (I).** Three or more ridges inside the right delta
- **Meet (M):** If the tracing of the ridge starts from the left delta and is followed to the right delta or nearest to it with one or two intervening ridges between the delta and the traced ridge. Fewer than three inside or outside right delta (0, 1, 2)
- **Outer (O):** If the ridge tracing followed near the right delta's relative point above or below with three or more intervening ridges between such delta and traced ridge. It is called an **OUTER (O).** Three or more ridges outside the right delta
- In accidental and double loop whorls, when the tracing passes inside of the right delta, stop at the nearest point to the right delta on the upward trend.

Observation:

Fingerprint whorl samples	Type of ridge tracing
	I, M, O???

RESULT

In the given fingerprint pattern, the Ridge tracing was successfully performed.

FORENSIC SIGNIFICANCE

Ridge tracing in whorl pattern analysis is a fundamental skill in forensic science. By following the prescribed procedures outlined in this manual, forensic experts can accurately count ridges and utilise this information in fingerprint identification and classification processes.

VIVA QUESTIONS

1. What is the first step in ridge tracing in fingerprint analysis?
2. How many core points can be present in a fingerprint?
3. What is the purpose of ridge tracing in fingerprint identification?
4. Which direction should you trace the ridges from the core point?
5. What happens when a ridge ends or meets another ridge?
6. How do you mark the next ridge to trace when encountering a bifurcation?
7. What is the term for the process of following a ridge from one point to another?
8. Can ridge tracing start from any point on the fingerprint?
9. How do you handle a situation where a ridge meets a scar or a crease?
10. What is the purpose of marking the ridges as "traced" during ridge tracing?
11. How do you determine the orientation of the ridges in a fingerprint?
12. What is the term for the point where a ridge meets a valley?
13. How do you handle a situation where two ridges merge into one?
14. What is the benefit of using a magnifying glass or loupe during ridge tracing?
15. How do you verify the accuracy of ridge tracing in fingerprint analysis?

CASE STUDIES

6

TO PERFORM PRIMARY CLASSIFICATION OF FINGERPRINTS

AIM

To perform Primary classification of fingerprints.

THEORY

Fingerprints are one of the most reliable forms of biometric identification, widely used in forensic investigations and security systems. The primary classification of fingerprints is a fundamental step in fingerprint analysis, which involves categorizing fingerprints into one of several pattern types, such as loops, whorls, and arches.

Classification of fingerprints is a method by which a set of fingerprints may be suitably filed in a filing system and easily retrieved for future use. The classification system used in all parts of the country and elsewhere is based on the basic Henry system. The classification formulae consist of letters and numbers arranged in the form of a fraction with a numerator and denominator. The formula is based on a study of the ten fingerprints of an individual. Each individual pattern is first identified and marked on the slip. Then, the classification formula is worked in a logical order in the following different steps:

(a) Primary classification

(b) Secondary classification

(c) Sub-secondary classification

(d) Final classification

PROCEDURE

1. Primary classification: To arrive at a primary classification, patterns are first divided into numerical and non-numerical patterns. Whorl and composite patterns are numerical patterns, whereas arches and loops are non-numerical patterns.
2. All the rolled impressions are numbered, on a fingerprint slip, from one to ten in the following order - 1-right thumb; 2- right index; 3-right middle finger; 4-right ring finger; 5-right little finger; 6-left thumb; 7-left index; 8-left middle finger; 9-left ring finger; and 10- left little finger.
3. Numerical values are assigned to the fingers in the following order. The first two (i.e., 1 and 2) positions of fingers are assigned value 16 each: 3 and 4 are assigned value 8 each; 5 & 6 are assigned value 4 each; 7 & 8 are assigned value 2 each; 9 & 10 are assigned value 1 each.
4. If the patterns identified come under numerical pattern group (i.e. whorls, composite), then the value assigned will be taken into account. If the patterns identified come under non-numerical pattern group (i.e. arches and loops), then the value assigned to these positions will not be taken into account and will be taken as 0 (zero).
5. After assigning the values, the values obtained for all the even-numbered fingers are placed in the numerator, and the values obtained for all the odd-numbered fingers are placed in the denominator. To obtain the primary classification, all values in the numerator are totaled, and 1 is added.
6. Similarly, all values in the denominator are totaled, and 1 is added. The fraction thus obtained constitutes the primary classification. The reason for adding 1 to both the numerator and denominator is to obtain a formula consisting of at least 1/1 rather than 0/0.

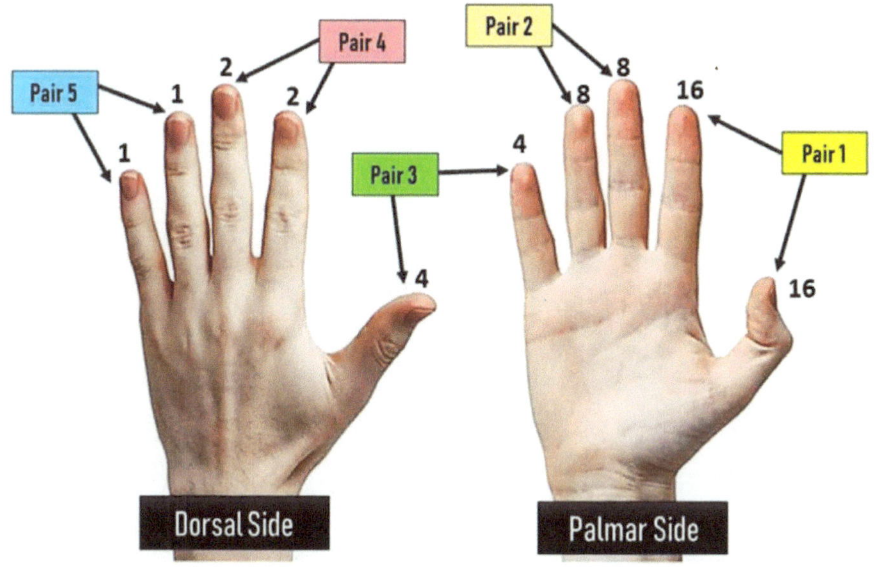

OBSERVATION

i. *Stick the sample on the blank side*

ii. *Calculate the value for primary classification*

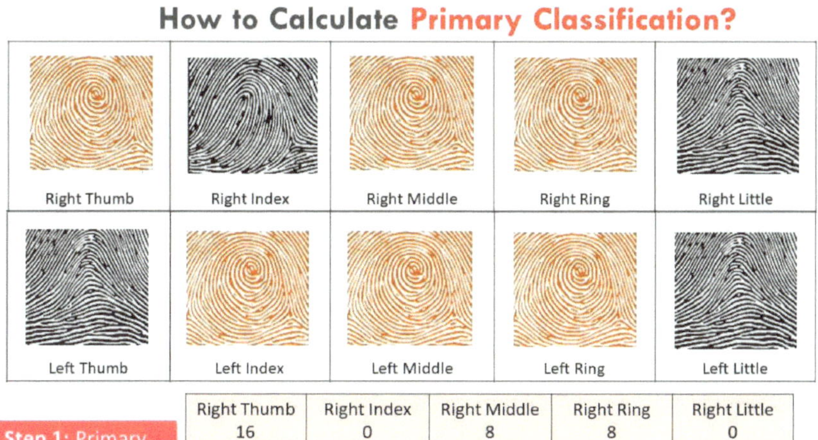

Step 1: Primary Values w.r.t. Whorls

Right Thumb 16	Right Index 0	Right Middle 8	Right Ring 8	Right Little 0
Left Thumb 0	Left Index 2	Left Middle 2	Left Ring 1	Left Little 0

• Formula for Primary classification :-

$$\text{P.C.} = \frac{\text{sum of even no. of finger(s)} \quad +1}{\text{sum of odd no. of finger(s)} \quad +1}$$

$$\text{P.C.} = \frac{2 + 4 + 6 + 8 + 10 + 1}{1 + 3 + 5 + 7 + 9 + 1}$$

FORENSIC SIGNIFICANCE

Classification of fingerprints is a method by which a set of fingerprints may be suitably filed in a filing system and easily retrieved for future use. The classification system used in all parts of the country and elsewhere is based on the basic Henry system.

RESULT

The primary classification of the given fingerprint sample was successfully performed.

VIVA QUESTIONS

1. What is the purpose of primary classification in fingerprint analysis?
2. How many main categories are fingerprints divided into for primary classification?
3. What are the three main types of fingerprint patterns used in primary classification?
4. How is the "loop" pattern distinguished from other patterns in primary classification?
5. What is the difference between a "radial" and an "ulnar" loop in primary classification?
6. How is the "whorl" pattern identified in primary classification?
7. What is the difference between a "plain arch" and a "tented arch" in primary classification?
8. How many fingers are typically classified in primary classification?
9. What is the purpose of assigning a "type" to each finger in primary classification?
10. How is the "key" or "core" point determined in primary classification?
11. What is the significance of the "delta" point in primary classification?
12. How are fingerprints with multiple patterns classified in primary classification?
13. What is the purpose of creating a "primary classification formula"?
14. How is the "primary classification index" used in fingerprint analysis?
15. What is the benefit of using primary classification in fingerprint identification?

CASE STUDIES

7

TO PERFORM SECONDARY AND SUB SECONDARY CLASSIFICATION IN THE GIVEN FINGERPRINT SAMPLES

AIM

To perform Secondary and sub secondary classification in the given fingerprint samples.

MATERIALS REQUIRED

Blank paper, fingerprint ink, roller, slab etc.

THEORY

Secondary classification

The secondary classification subdivides large groups of fingerprint slips having the same primary classification. The secondary classification consists of capital letter symbols for the patterns of the two index fingers, with the right index finger symbol appearing in the numerator and the left index symbol in the denominator. The five basic pattern types that can appear on index fingers are arch (A), tented arch (T), radial loop (R), ulnar loop (U), and whorl (W). For the purpose of this classification, composite patterns are classified as plain whorl under the symbol (W). As many as 25 possible combinations are possible out of this classification.

Sub-secondary classification

The sub-secondary classification further subdivides large groups having the same primary and secondary classification. The sub-secondary classification is represented by symbols that may be 1, M, or O. These symbols are given to the index, middle, and ring fingers of the right hand and make up the numerator; the same left fingers for the left- hand make up the denominator. These symbols are derived from the ridge tracing of the whorls appearing on the index, middle, and ring fingers or from ridge counts of loops on those fingers.

PROCEDURE

For Secondary classification

1) All Patterns on Index Fingers are considered
2) They are designated by CAPITAL LETTERS.
3) In general, the following are the most commonly encountered pattern types:
    - Plain arch (A)
    - Tented arch (T)
    - Ulnar loop (U)
    - Radial loop (R)
    - Whorl (W)
4) Once the fingerprint patterns are identified on the index fingers, they are classified under the classification, and the observation is written.
5) Right hand (index finger) Left hand (index finger)

For sub - secondary classification

6) Ridge counting and tracing for loops and whorls
7) Fingers Included: Index, middle, and ring fingers.
8) Numerical values are assigned in corresponding words.

9) Letter designation for ridge counting of loops

- Index Finger: inner (I) = 1 to 9
- Outer (O) = 9+
- Middle Finger: Inner (I) = 1 to 10
- Outer (O) = 10+
- Ring Finger: Inner (I) = 1 to 13
- Outer (O) = 13+

10) Letter Designation for Ridge tracing for whorls

- Meet (M) = 0,1 or 2 ridges inside or outside the right delta
- Inner (I) = 3 or more inside the right delta.
- Outer (O) = 3 or more outside the right delta

11) **Formula:**

- Numerator = Ridge counting/tracing value of right hand
- Denominator = Ridge counting/tracing value of left hand

OBSERVATION

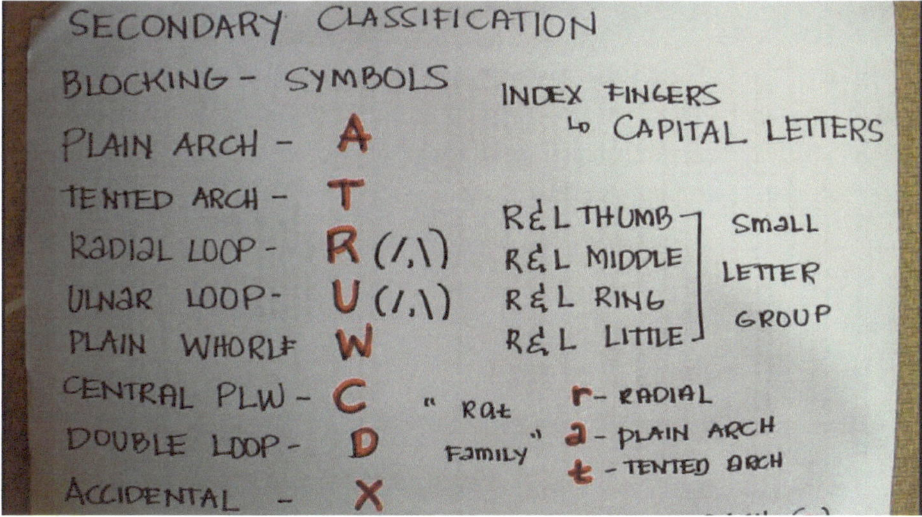

SUB-SECONDARY CLASSIFICATION
RIDGE COUNTING - LOOPS
WHORL TRACING - WHORLS
NOT INCLUDED - ARCHES (DASH -)
INDEX - MIDDLE - RING
LOOPS
INDEX
1-9 INNER "I"
10 or more OUTER "O"
MIDDLE
1-10 INNER "I"
11 or more OUTER "O"
WHORLS
I - INNER - 3 or more RIDGES INSIDE / ABOVE
O - OUTER - 3 or more RIDGES OUTSIDE / BELOW
M - MEETING - MEET EXACTLY (O)

RESULT

The secondary and sub-secondary classification was successfully performed.

FORENSIC SIGNIFICANCE

Classification of fingerprints is a method by which a set of fingerprints may be suitably filed in a filing system and easily retrieved for future use. The classification system used in all parts of the country and elsewhere is based on the basic Henry system.

VIVA QUESTIONS

1. What is the purpose of secondary classification in fingerprint analysis?
2. How many secondary classification divisions are there in the Henry System?
3. What is the difference between a “hyped” and “type” classification in secondary classification?
4. How are fingerprints with a “loop” pattern further classified in secondary classification?

5. What is the significance of the "sub-secondary" classification in fingerprint analysis?
6. How are fingerprints with a "whorl" pattern further classified in secondary classification?
7. What is the purpose of assigning a "sub-secondary" classification to a fingerprint?
8. How many sub-secondary classification divisions are there in the Henry System?
9. What is the difference between a "Lyon" and "Lyu" sub-secondary classification?
10. How are fingerprints with a "tented arch" pattern further classified in secondary classification?
11. What is the significance of the "delta" point in secondary classification?
12. How are fingerprints with multiple patterns classified in secondary classification?
13. What is the purpose of creating a "secondary classification formula"?
14. How is the "secondary classification index" used in fingerprint analysis?
15. What is the benefit of using secondary and sub-secondary classification in fingerprint identification?

CASE STUDIES

8

TO PERFORM FINAL AND KEY CLASSIFICATION OF GIVEN FINGERPRINT SAMPLE

AIM

To perform final and key classification of given fingerprint sample

THEORY:

To understand and apply the final and key classification steps in the fingerprint analysis process, enhancing the ability to systematically categorise fingerprint patterns. The final classification in fingerprint analysis involves determining the ridge counts of loops and the complexity of whorls. This step is crucial for accurately categorizing and comparing fingerprints. Ridge counts are taken between the delta and the core for loops, while whorls are assessed for their ridge count on both sides of the core. The final classification helps refine the categorization process by providing detailed, quantifiable data on each fingerprint pattern.

Key classification, on the other hand, focuses on a specific finger, often the right index finger, to determine a key value. This value is derived from the ridge count or pattern complexity of the identified key finger. The key classification provides a simplified yet vital identifier that assists in the quick retrieval and comparison of fingerprint records within a larger database. Together, the final and key classifications enhance the precision and efficiency of fingerprint analysis in forensic investigations.

MATERIALS

- Fingerprint ink pad
- Fingerprint cards or plain white paper
- Magnifying glass
- Ruler
- Pencil and eraser
- Reference chart of fingerprint patterns (loops, whorls, and arches)
- Clean cloth or wipes

PROCEDURE

Part 1: Collecting Fingerprint Samples

1. **Preparation:**
   - Clean your hands thoroughly to remove any dirt or oils.
   - Dry your hands completely.
2. **Inking the Fingers:**
   - Lightly press the pad of each finger onto the ink pad, ensuring an even coat of ink.
   - Roll the finger from one side to the other on the fingerprint card or paper, starting with the thumb of the right hand and working through to the little finger of the left hand.
3. **Recording the Prints:**

- Ensure each fingerprint is clear and distinct. Label the fingerprints with the corresponding finger names (e.g., "Right Thumb," "Left Index," etc.).

4. **Cleaning Up:**
   - Use a clean cloth or wipes to remove ink from your fingers.

Part 2: Analyzing and Classifying Fingerprints

1. **Identify Fingerprint Patterns:**
   - Identify the pattern type for each fingerprint (loop, whorl, or arch).

Part 3: Final Classification

1. **Determining Ridge Counts:**
   - For loops, count the number of ridges between the delta and the core of the fingerprint.
   - For whorls, identify the ridge count on both the left and right sides of the core.
2. **Assign Final Classification:**
   - The final classification is usually based on the ridge counts of the loops and the presence of whorls. Record the ridge count for loops and use the reference chart to assign a numerical value for whorls.
   - If multiple whorls are present, consider the most complex pattern or use the average ridge count if needed.
3. average ridge count if needed.

Final Classification

Henry Classification Number

	Key	Major	Primary	Secondary	SubSecondary	Final
CLASS	9	M	17	W	IOM	10
		L	1	U	000	

Rules

1. **Fingers:** Little fingers of one hand
2. **Patterns:** Loops (or Whorls)
3. **Values:** Ridge counting for loops (and also for whorls)
4. **Numerator=** Right hand
5. ***Denominator=** Left hand
6. ***Preference:** Right little finger, if doesn't have loops left little finger.
7. **If Loops are absent:** Whorl (treated as ulnar loop)
    - **Whorl on right hand=** Counted from left delta to core
    - **Left hand=** Counted from right delta to core

Final Classification: #1 Practice

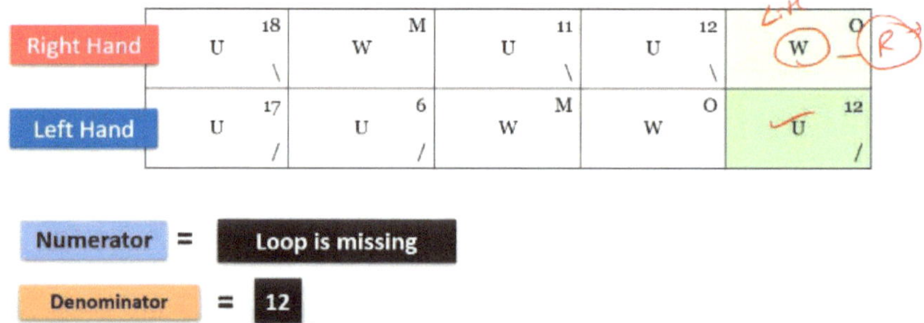

Right Hand	U 18 \	W M	U 11 \	U 12 \	W O
Left Hand	U 17 /	U 6 /	W M	W O	U 12 /

Numerator = Loop is missing

Denominator = 12

Part 4: Key Classification

1. **Identify the Key Finger:**
    - The key classification is typically derived from the fingerprint pattern on a specific finger, often the right index finger. However, the key finger may vary based on different classification systems.
2. **Assign Key Value:**
    - For the identified key finger, note its pattern type and ridge count.
    - Use the reference chart to convert the ridge count or pattern complexity into a numerical key value.

Key Classification of Fingerprint

Henry Classification Number

	Key	Major	Primary	Secondary	SubSecondary	Final
CLASS	9	M	17	W	IOM	10
		L	1	U	OOO	

Rules

1. Values sit at front of Henry Classification
2. Ridge count the first loop that is appearing on the card.
3. **Exception:** Loops on little finger.
4. **Values:** only in the numerator.

Key Classification: #1 Practice

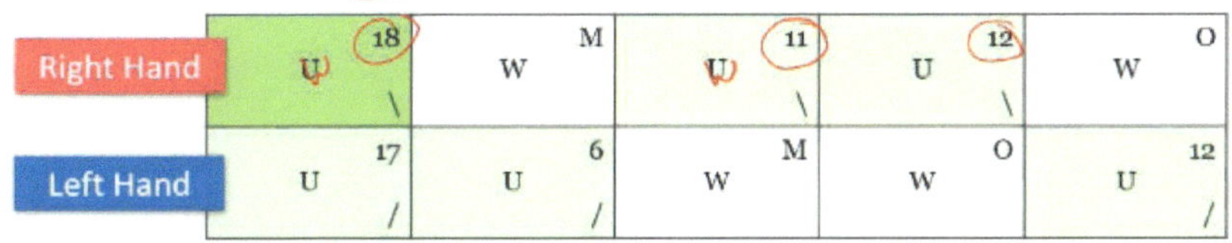

Right Hand	U 18 \	W M	U 11 \	U 12 \	W O
Left Hand	U 17 /	U 6 /	W M	W O	U 12 /

Numerator (Ridge count of first loop in the card) = **18**

Data Analysis and Interpretation

- **Final Classification Example:**
  - Suppose the right index finger has a loop with a ridge count of 12.
  - The right thumb has a whorl with a value of 16.

  Final Classification: Loop with ridge count of 12 on the right index, whorl with a value of 16 on the right thumb.
- **Key Classification Example:**
  - Using the right index finger as the key finger with a ridge count of 12, assign the numerical key value based on the reference chart.

OBSERVATION:

Henry Classification Number

					LLL (Second LMM SubSecondary)	
CLASS	15	M	1	U	000	16
		M	1	U	000	
	Key	Major	Primary	Secondary	SubSecondary	Final

This is Henry classification value chart where you have to put value for final and key classification.

CONCLUSION

Summarise the process of final and key classification in fingerprint analysis. Discuss how these classifications contribute to the systematic categorization and identification of fingerprints. Reflect on the ease or difficulty of determining ridge counts and assigning classification values.

Viva Questions:

1. How does the ridge count of loops affect the final classification?
2. What challenges did you face while counting ridges and identifying patterns?
3. How might the final and key classification steps be utilised in real-world forensic investigations?
4. How are fingerprint patterns classified?
5. What is the role of minutiae in fingerprint comparison?
6. Describe the process of determining the ridge count for a loop pattern.
7. How would you assign a numerical value to a whorl pattern during final classification?

8. If you identify a loop on the right index finger, what steps would you take to calculate its ridge count?
9. How do you use the ridge count of a fingerprint to derive the final classification?
10. Explain the procedure for identifying the key value from a key finger in the classification process.

CASE STUDIES

9

COMPARISON BETWEEN TWO FINGERPRINT SAMPLES

AIM

To compare two given fingerprint samples.

THEORY

The palmar surface of the hands, as well as the soles of the feet, found both in men and monkeys, are enclosed with minute ridges that possess a superficial resemblance to those made on the sand by wind or flowing water. The ridges are subject to certain breaks or interruptions, presenting various kinds of characteristics referred to as minutiae. These minutiae are able to describe the invariant and discriminatory details and are helpful in identifying fingerprints. The friction ridges have certain basic features, which are present in sufficient numbers in every fingerprint. These minutiae can be easily identified based on their shape or appearance. Each and every fingerprint comprises these ridge characteristics, though it is their sequence that makes a fingerprint unique. They are also sometimes referred to as Galton's details. Sir Francis Galton was the first one to notice that the ridges on the fingers do not path in line without breaking, and he identified numerous ridge characteristics to support the identification of the fingerprints.

Types of Ridge Characteristics

Following are the main types of ridge characteristics or minutiae:

1. **Ridge ending:** This is a ridge, which abruptly ends its path. They occur very abundantly in a finger impression.
2. **Bifurcation:** It is a ridge, which splits into two small ridges forming a Y shape. It is also known as diverging fork. They give an appearance of branch points between curved lines. These are also encountered very frequently in a fingerprint.
3. **Trifurcation:** It is a ridge, which splits into three small ridges. It is rare in occurrence.
4. **Interjunction:** It is the joining of two adjacent ridges by a short diagonal ridge. It is also called a crossover.
5. **Fragment/ Short Ridge:** It is an independent ridge of relatively small length.
6. **Enclosure/Lake:** It is a ridge that first bifurcates and then converges or joins back to form an elliptical enclosure. It is also called a lake. It can vary in size.
7. **Island:** It is a point or a dot within the overall pattern of a fingerprint.
8. **Intersection /Change Over** It is formed when two adjacent ridges change their places by crossing over each other.
9. **Return:** It is a ridge that changes its path and takes a U-turn.
10. **Hook/ Spur:** When a small curved ridge, which is attached to the main ridge, forms a hook or spur-like appearance.

Requirements

Fingerprint samples; magnifying glass.

PROCEDURE

1. Two Fingerprint samples were provided, and the fingerprint patterns were determined.
2. Minutiae were identified with respect to their locations from both fingerprint samples.
3. A comparison is made between two fingerprints and recorded in the observation table.

Samples

Paste two fingerprint samples on the left side

OBSERVATION TABLE

Fingerprint 1	Fingerprint 2
Mention 1. Fingerprint Pattern 2. Ridge characteristics with their respective locations	Mention 1. Fingerprint Pattern 2. Ridge characteristics with their respective locations

RESULT

Based on comparison of ridge characteristics, two fingerprint samples are same/ two fingerprint samples are different. A minimum of 8 minutiae are needed to make a match between two fingerprints samples. In the given sample, 8 minutiae of fingerprint 1 is matching with the fingerprint 2. Hence, it can be concluded that, both fingerprints are from the same person.

FORENSIC SIGNIFICANCE

1. Ridge characteristics or minutiae are able to capture invariant and discriminatory information and are used to identify fingerprints.
2. The individuality of any fingerprint is based not upon the general shape or pattern that it forms but instead upon its ridge structure and its specific characteristics (also known as minutiae).

3. The number and locations of the minutiae vary from finger to finger in any particular person and from person to person for any particular finger.
4. If minimum of 8 ridge characteristics are same in two prints, they are said to have common source.

Precautions

1. Fingerprint samples should be handled properly. It should not be handled on the ink part.

VIVA QUESTIONS

1. What is the purpose of comparing two fingerprint samples?
2. What is the first step in comparing two fingerprint samples?
3. How many points of comparison are needed to confirm a match?
4. What are the three main patterns found in fingerprints?
5. How are fingerprint patterns classified?
6. What is the role of minutiae in fingerprint comparison?
7. How many types of minutiae are there in fingerprints?
8. Can identical twins have the same fingerprints?
9. How accurate is fingerprint comparison?
10. What software is used for fingerprint comparison?
11. Can fingerprints change over time?
12. How are fingerprint comparisons used in forensic science?
13. Can fingerprints be altered or tampered with?
14. How are fingerprint comparisons used in border control?
15. Are fingerprint comparisons admissible in court?

CASE STUDIES

10

TO INVESTIGATE PHYSICAL METHODS OF FINGERPRINT DETECTION

AIM

To identify and record the non-porous latent fingerprints of your family members (from a cell phone, door, table, etc.) at home using **PHYSICAL METHODS** of fingerprint detection and study the type of fingerprint and ridge characteristics.

PRINCIPLE

Fingerprints are especially important in the criminal justice realm. Investigators and analysts can compare unknown prints collected from a crime scene to the known prints of victims, witnesses and potential suspects to assist in criminal cases.

For example:

- A killer may leave the fingerprints on the suspected murder weapon
- A bank robber's fingerprint may be found on a robbery note
- In an assault case, the perpetrator may have left fingerprints on the victim's skin
- A burglar may leave fingerprints on a broken windowpane
- A thief's fingerprint may be found on a safe

In addition, fingerprints can link a perpetrator to other unsolved crimes if investigators have reason. Compare them or see if prints from an unsolved crime turn up as a match during a database search. Sometimes, these unknown prints linking multiple crimes can help investigators piece together enough information to zero in on the culprit.

Fingerprints can be found on practically any solid surface, including the human body. Analysts classify fingerprints into three categories according to the type of surface on which they are found and whether they are visible or not: **Fingerprints on soft surfaces (such as soap, wax, wet paint, fresh caulk, etc.) are likely to be three-dimensional plastic prints; those on hard surfaces are either patent (visible) or latent (invisible) prints.** Visible prints are formed when blood, dirt, ink, paint, etc., is transferred from a finger or thumb to a surface. Patent prints can be found on a wide variety of surfaces: smooth or rough, porous (such as paper, cloth, or wood), or non-porous (such as metal, glass, or plastic).

Latent prints are formed when the body's natural oils and sweat on the skin are deposited onto another surface. Latent prints can be found on a variety of surfaces; however, they are not readily visible and detection often requires the use of **fingerprint powders, chemical reagents or alternate light sources**. Generally speaking, the smoother and less porous a surface is, the greater the potential that any latent prints present can be found and developed.

PROCEDURE

Collecting Latent Prints

One of the most common methods for discovering and collecting latent fingerprints is by dusting a smooth or non-porous surface with fingerprint powder ***(black granular, aluminum flake, black magnetic, etc.)***. If any prints appear, they are photographed and then lifted from the surface with clear adhesive tape. However, fingerprint powders can contaminate the evidence and ruin the opportunity to perform other techniques that could turn up a hidden print or additional information. Therefore, investigators may examine the area with an alternate light source or apply ***cyanoacrylate (super glue)*** before using powders.

1. Black Powder

Black powder is used to process the sticky side of adhesive tapes and labels for latent prints. This method is particularly useful on dark-coloured and black tape.

MATERIALS AND EQUIPMENT'S REQUIRED

- Laboratory coat and gloves
- Magnetic stirrer, magnetic follower, and magnetic retriever
- Glass beakers
- Graduated cylinders
- Dark, shatter-proof container
- Forceps (soft-tipped)
- Glass trays
- Camera/scanner
- Petri or shallow dish, small brush, or fingerprint kit

Chemicals

- Black powder – 1 tablespoon
- Solvent – Petroleum ether

Mixing Procedure

Place the black powder in a Petri or shallow dish. Add solvent to the powder and stir until the mixture is consistent with thin paint.

Processing Procedure

The solution is painted on the adhesive surface of the tape with a camel hair or small brush. Allow to set for 30 to 60 seconds, then rinse off the solution with a slow stream of cold tap water. Allow to dry. Repeat the procedure if necessary.

Fingerprint Powders

Black Powder

Application of black powder and subsequent magnification

2. Alternate Light Source (ALS)

It is becoming more commonplace for investigators to examine any likely surfaces (doors, doorknobs, windows, railings, etc.) with an alternate light source. These are laser or LED devices that emit a particular wavelength, or spectrum, of light. Some devices have different filters to provide a variety of spectra that can be photographed or further processed with powders or dye stains. For example, investigators may use a ***blue light with an orange filter to find latent prints on desks, chairs, computer equipment, or other objects at the scene of a break-in***.

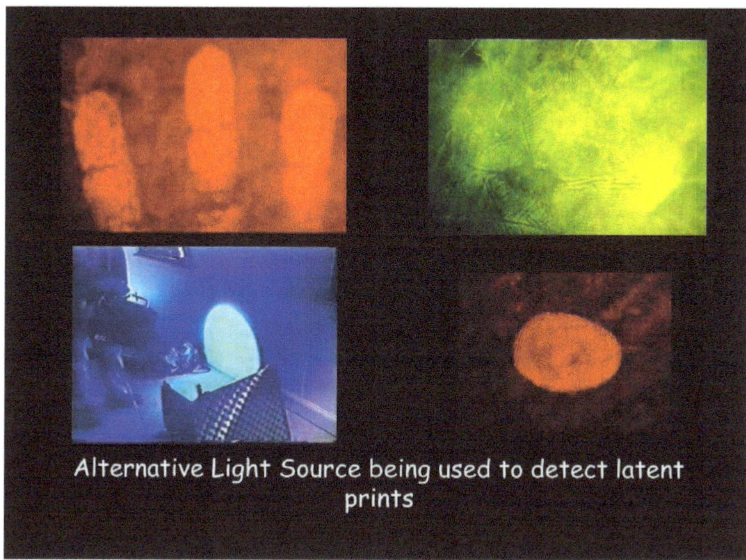

Alternative Light Source being used to detect latent prints

RESULT

1. Give the photograph of a minimum of 3 fingerprints taken by any one of the above methods.
2. Categorise the three fingerprints as they are given in the table.

Sl. No	Finger print	Label	Ridge Characteristic
1			
2			
3			

VIVA QUESTIONS

1. Identical twins have the same fingerprints. (T/F)
2. The three basic types of fingerprint patterns are:
   a. Arches, loops, and rings.
   b. Whorls, arches, and accidentals.
   c. Whorls, accidentals, and loops.
   d. Loops, arches, and whorls.
3. Which of the following is *not* one of the features that must be present in order for a fingerprint pattern to be classified as a loop pattern?
   a. A single delta.
   b. A Core
   c. A minimum ridge count of one
   d. A ridge ending.

4. Name all possible physical methods to develop latent fingerprints.
5. Which of the following fingerprint visualization techniques is particularly effective on paper that has been wet, materials soaked in petrol, and chip wrappers?
   a. Sudan Black.
   b. Superglue fuming.
   c. Physical developer.
   d. Gentian Violet.
6. The latent fingerprint visualization technique known as vacuum metal deposition involves the evaporation and subsequent deposition, under vacuum, of:
   a. Gold and/or silver.
   b. Zinc and/or silver.
   c. Copper and/or gold.
   d. Silver and/or gold
7. The dark portion of the fingerprint is called the ________.
   a. Valley
   b. Delta
   c. Core
   d. Ridge
8. The skin layer between the epidermis and dermis is the ________ layer
   a. Basal
   b. Cuticle
   c. Subcutaneous
9. Which physical method would you employ to detect the fingerprints on porous and non-porous surfaces?
10. Fingerprint patterns that can eliminate a suspect or link a suspect to the crime scene
    a. Minutia

b. Palm Prints

c. Hand Prints

d. Retinal scanner

11. What is the most common physical method of fingerprint detection?
12. How does powder dusting enhance fingerprint visibility?
13. What is the purpose of using a brush in powder dusting?
14. How does the chemical composition of superglue (cyanoacrylate) help in fingerprint detection?
15. What is the principle behind using ninhydrin to detect fingerprints?
16. How does the use of ultraviolet (UV) light aid in fingerprint detection?
17. What is the purpose of using a luminol solution in fingerprint detection?
18. How does the use of fingerprint tape or lifting tape aid in evidence collection?
19. What is the difference between a visible and latent fingerprint?
20. How does the physical method of fingerprint detection using iodine crystals work?

At HOME - *Finger Print from a Light Surface*

1. Talcum Powder
2. Create a Charcoal – burn something and get the materials or a nearby Ironing man

CASE STUDIES

11

TO INVESTIGATE CHEMICAL METHODS OF FINGERPRINT DETECTION

AIM

To identify and record the non-porous latent fingerprint of your family members (from a cell phone, or door or table etc.) at home by **CHEMICAL METHODS** of fingerprint detection and study the type of fingerprint and ridge characteristics.

PRINCIPLE

Three types of fingerprints can be found at a crime scene—plastic, visible, and latent. **Plastic impressions** are fingerprints left in soft materials such as butter, soap, and putty. **Visible prints** are prints made when fingers are covered in a substance like blood, dirt, or paint, which leaves a mark on a surface. **Latent prints** are not visible to the human eye and are formed when sweat and natural body oils make contact with another surface. Through a process called latent print development, you can make these prints visible. Developing latent prints involves either a **chemical or physical process** using alternate light sources, fingerprint powders, or, in this case, chemical reagents. *Whatever tool you use should react with the skin secretions, causing the latent print to stand out against its background.*

Choosing the right tool requires some understanding of the chemical makeup of the fingerprint. Most latent fingerprints consist of **secretions of**

the skin's glands. Three types of glands are responsible for these secretions: **the eccrine glands, the sebaceous glands, and the apocrine glands.** Sebaceous glands are not present in the hands, but secretions from these glands are transferred to the hands by touching areas where these glands are present, such as the hair and face.

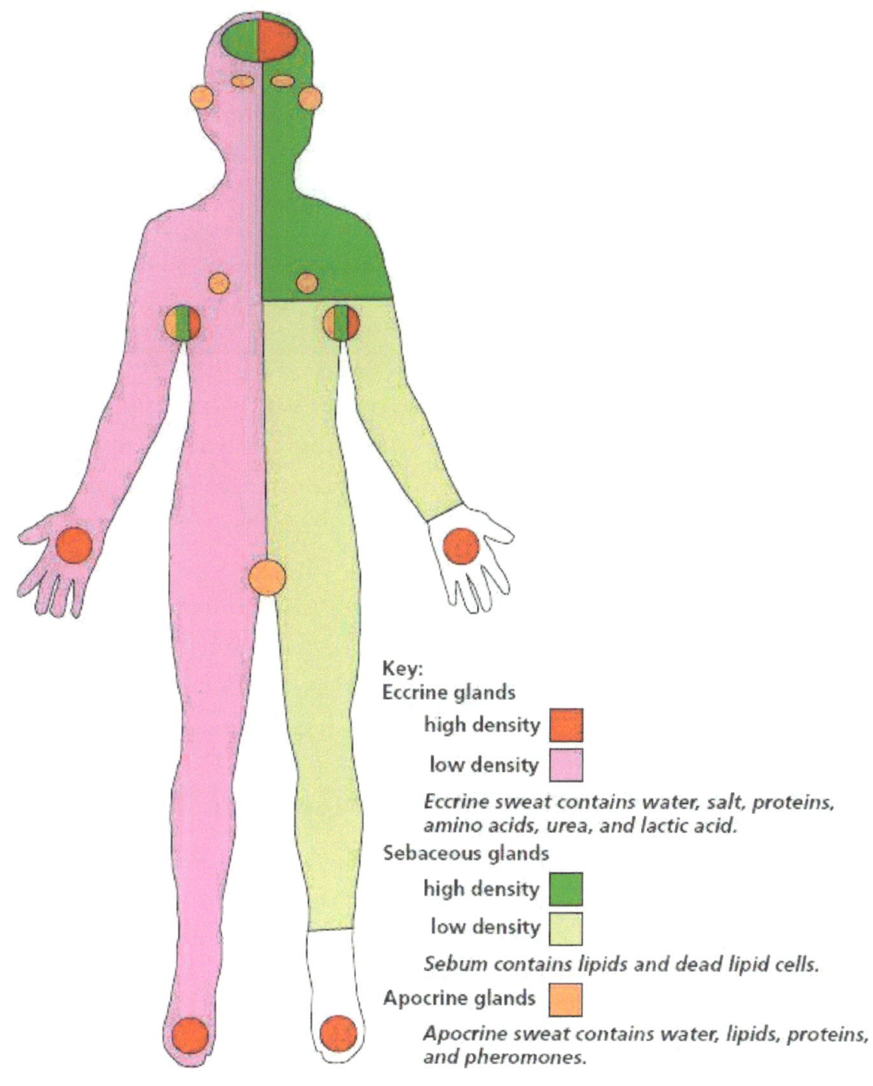

Primary locations of eccrine, sebaceous, and apocrine glands on the human body.

PROCEDURE

Collecting Latent Prints

One of the most common methods for discovering and collecting latent fingerprints is by dusting a smooth or nonporous surface with fingerprint powder **(black granular, aluminum flake, black magnetic, etc.).** If any prints appear, they are photographed and then lifted from the surface with clear adhesive tape. However, fingerprint powders can contaminate the evidence and ruin the opportunity to perform other techniques that could turn up a hidden print or additional information. Therefore, investigators may examine the area with an alternate light source or apply **cyanoacrylate (super glue)** before using powders.

Chemical Developers

Porous surfaces such as paper and wood are typically processed with chemicals, including **cyanoacrylate (superglue) ninhydrin, silver nitrate, iodine**, and physical developer, to reveal latent fingerprints. These chemicals react with specific components of latent print residue, such as amino acids and inorganic salts. Silver nitrate (AgNO3) reacts with the chlorides in skin secretions to form silver chloride, which turns gray when exposed to UV light. Developed prints must be photographed immediately because the reaction will eventually (and permanently) fill the background. Silver nitrate is useful on paper, cardboard, plastics, and unvarnished, light-coloured woods. **It is not useful on items that have been exposed to water.**

1. Development of Latent Fingerprints with cyanoacrylate

Investigators often perform cyanoacrylate (superglue) processing, **or fuming, of a surface before applying powders or dye stains**. This process, typically performed on non-porous surfaces, involves exposing the object to cyanoacrylate vapors. The vapors (fumes) will adhere to any prints present on the object, allowing them to be viewed with oblique *ambient light or a white light source.*

Latent Prints on a Pistol	The needed components	The Chemical Formula
	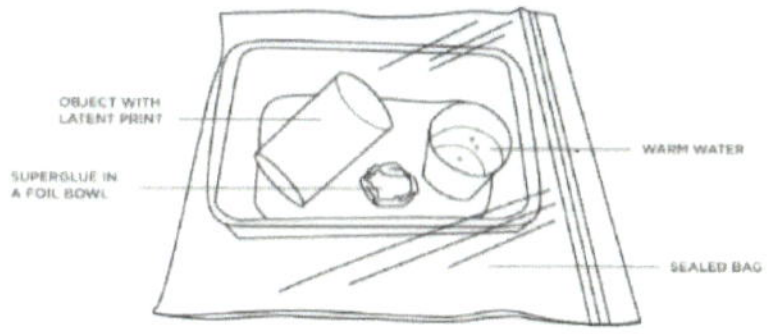	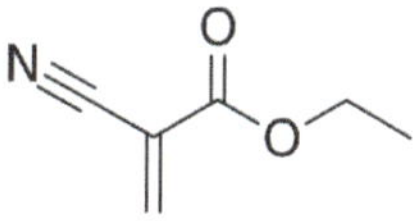

2. Development of Latent Fingerprints with Silver Nitrate

Safety

Avoid contact with silver nitrate, as it can discolour skin and clothing. Wear gloves, goggles, and an apron when handling the silver nitrate solution.

MATERIALS

- Silver Nitrate Solution, 3% (0.75 g AgNO3 in 25 mL water; contained in a spray bottle)
- Copy paper (1 sheet per student)
- Newspaper (or other covering to collect overspray)
- Pencils
- Personal Protective Equipment (PPE)

Preparation

Cover the lab surface with newspaper to collect overspray. Arrange for students to be able to expose their prints to direct sunlight, either by opening a window or by taking the paper outside.

PROCEDURE

1. Set up your evidence.
   a. Draw a horizontal line dividing a piece of paper in half. Write your initials or name in both pencil and pen in both the top half and the bottom half of the paper.

b. With your left hand, place several random fingerprints on the top half of the paper.

2. Allow the paper to dry and absorb the prints for 5 minutes. **Wear gloves for the remainder of the procedure**.
3. Place your paper on the work surface.
4. Hold the spray bottle containing the silver nitrate solution approximately 2 to 3 inches from the surface of the paper. Remember, this chemical reacts with skin, so avoid contact.
5. Spray from the upper left corner across the page and then move down the page, spraying until the sheet is saturated.
6. Allow the paper to dry for 1 minute.
7. Expose the paper to sunlight for 1 to 2 minutes. Once the prints begin to develop, remove the paper from the sunlight. Further exposure will continue to darken the prints and background.

Silver Nitrate Fingerprint

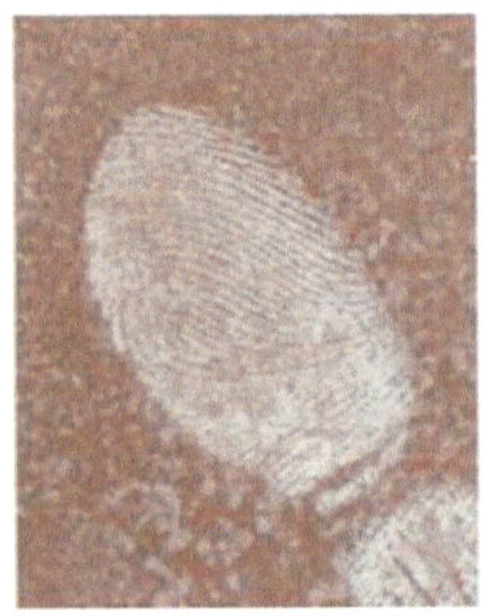

Silver Nitrate

VIVA

1. Sodium chloride (NaCl) is the chemical component of sweat that reacts with silver nitrate. Write the balanced equation for this reaction.
2. Latent prints are suspected on a surface, but none are found after treatment with silver nitrate. Describe which factors might contribute

to this discrepancy and explain the procedural steps you would take to ensure that all latent prints on the surface are developed.

3. What are the other chemical methods for developing fingerprints?

3. Iodine Fuming Method

Iodine fumes adhere to grease or oils on porous surfaces and appear as a yellow stain. ***Latent prints developed with iodine fumes must be photographed immediately.***

Equipment: Fuming chamber, ceramic or glass dish, heat source

Materials and Chemicals: Iodine (ACS reagent grade)

Processing Procedure

Place iodine crystals in the ceramic or glass dish and place the specimen to be processed in the fuming chamber. Apply heat to the crystals and observe development. Remove the specimen(s) from the chamber when sufficient development has occurred.

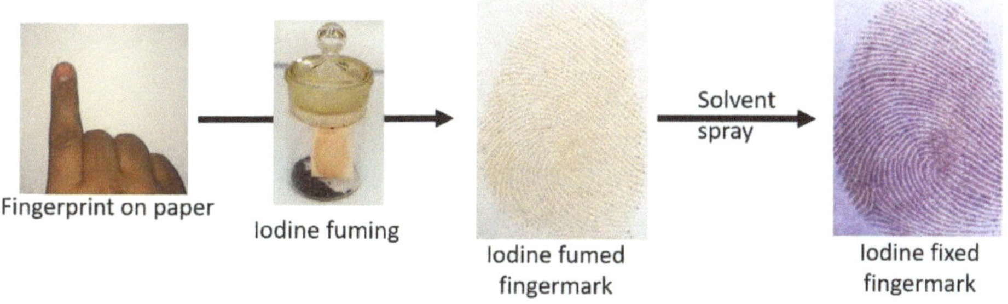

RESULT

1. Give the photograph of a minimum 3 fingerprints taken by developing using silver nitrate/ Iodine
2. Categorise the 3 fingerprints as they are given in the Table.

Sl.No	Finger print	Label	Ridge Characteristic
1			
2			
3			

At HOME - ***Finger Print from a Dark Surface***

1. Iodine (First Aid Kit)
2. Can get from a nearby medical store or a clinic

VIVA QUESTIONS:

1. What is the purpose of using chemical methods in fingerprint detection?
2. How does Ninhydrin react with amino acids in fingerprints?
3. What is the principle behind using cyanoacrylate (superglue) fuming in fingerprint detection?
4. How does the use of luminol reveal latent fingerprints?
5. What is the difference between a fluorescent and chemiluminescent reaction in fingerprint detection?
6. How does the use of diaza-9-fluorenol (DFO) help in detecting fingerprints?
7. What is the purpose of using 1,2-diaza-9-fluorenol (1,2-DFO) in fingerprint detection?
8. How does the use of zinc chloride help in detecting fingerprints?

9. What is the principle behind using physical developer (PD) in fingerprint detection?
10. How does the use of oil red O (ORO) help in detecting fingerprints?
11. What is the difference between a lipid-based and amino acid-based fingerprint detection method?
12. How does the use of Nile red help in detecting fingerprints?
13. What is the purpose of using a fixative in chemical fingerprint detection methods?
14. How does the use of a counterstain enhance fingerprint visibility?
15. What is the importance of using a control sample in chemical fingerprint detection methods?

CASE STUDIES

12

LIP PRINTS

AIM

To classify and identify the lip prints.

MATERIAL REQUIRED

A4 paper, magnifying glass, lipstick, ruler, rencil etc

THEORY

Lips are two highly sensitive folds composed of skin, muscle, glands, and mucous membranes.

- *They surround the oral orifice and form the anterior boundary of the oral cavity*
- *Upper lip – from under the nose and extending laterally toward the cheeks from the nasolabial sulcus.*
- *Lower lip – bounded inferiorly by a prominent groove, the labiodental sulcus*

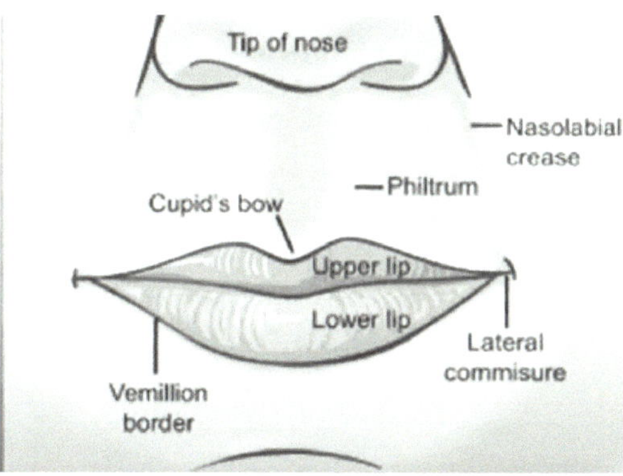

According to lip thickness, there are four groups.

- *Thin lips European caucasian*
- *Medium lips – most common (8-10mm)*
- *Thick or very thick lips – negroes*
- *Mix lips – orientals*

Cheiloscopy is a forensic investigation technique that deals with identification of humans based on lips traces. Lip prints have to be obtained within 24 hours of time of death to prevent erroneous data that would result from postmortem alterations of lip. Suzuki and Tsuchihashi divided the lips into four quadrants and formulated their own classification of 6 different types of grooves. They demonstrated that no two lip prints manifested the same pattern.

Suzuki and Tsuchihashi's Classification (1970)

- **Type I**: A complete lip print with well-defined features
- **IA**: A Type I lip print with a clear impression of the Cupid's bow (the curve of the lips)
- **IB**: A Type I lip print without a clear impression of the Cupid's bow.
- **Type II**: An incomplete lip print with some features missing
- **IIA**: A Type II lip print with a partial impression of the Cupid's bow.
- **IIB**: A Type II lip print without any impression of the Cupid's bow.
- **Type III**: A distorted lip print with unclear features
- **IIIA**: A Type III lip print with some features visible but distorted.
- **IIIB**: A Type III lip print with no visible features.
- **Type IV**: A lip print with unusual features or patterns
- **IVA**: A Type IV lip print with unique features or patterns on the upper lip.
- **IVB**: A Type IV lip print with unique features or patterns on the lower lip.

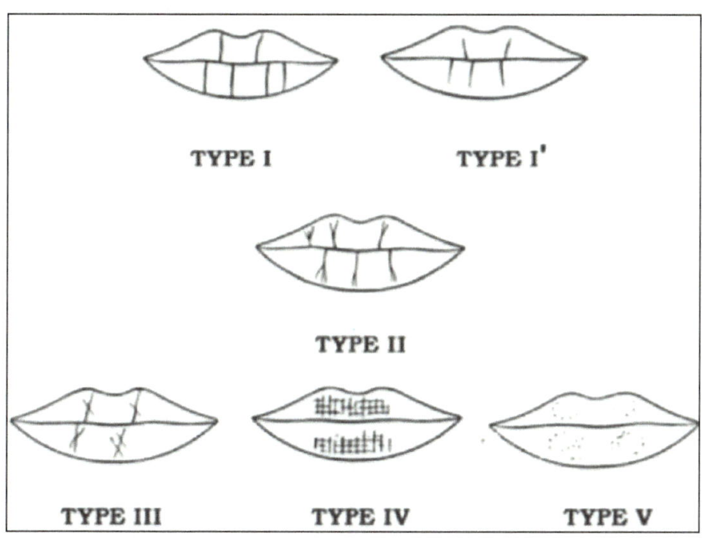

PROCEDURE

- Select the subject. Ensure the subject doesn't have any lip injuries, deformities, or lipstick allergies.
- Ask the subject to apply lipstick or lip gloss evenly on their lips.
- Instruct the subject to press their lips gently onto the paper. This creates a clear impression.
- Stick a transparent tape over the lip print for preservation.
- Divide and label the lip print into 4 quadrants.
- Use a magnifying glass or microscope to examine the lip print.
- Identify and note down any distinctive features such as grooves, furrows, and other patterns.

OBSERVATION TABLE

QUADRANT	TYPES

RESULT

The lip print analysis was done successfully.

VIVA QUESTIONS

1. What are lip prints?
2. How are lip prints formed?
3. Are lip prints unique like fingerprints?
4. What is the study of lip prints called?
5. How are lip prints collected?
6. What are the different types of lip prints?
7. How are lip prints used in forensic science?
8. Can lip prints be used for biometric identification?
9. How accurate are lip prints for identification?
10. Can lip prints be altered or changed?
11. How are lip prints analyzed?
12. What are the advantages of using lip prints for identification?
13. What are the limitations of using lip prints for identification?
14. Can lip prints be used in combination with other biometric identifiers?
15. What is the future of lip print analysis?

CASE STUDIES

13

CASTING OF FOOTPRINT

AIM

To prepare cast of footprints

MATERIALS REQUIRED

Casting kit, POP, wire mesh, distilled water, scale

THEORY

Footprints are the impressions left behind by a person walking or running. Footprints are pieces of impression evidence that can place a suspect at a crime scene based on unique shoe sizes or patterns. In footprints, the parameters that are taken into consideration are the dimensions of the stride, the footprint's location, its size and shape, the angulations, interspaces, deepness, the outer margins, creases in heels, information regarding the gait pattern from the injuries and accidental damages, length of legs and height of the individual range of body weight and interrelated movement of the foot, ankle, leg and the body that are individualistic to that particular person. Footprint can be of three types: Sunken footprint, surface print, and negative print. Footprint collection can be done using photography, tracing, lifting, and casting.

PROCEDURE

Preparation of plaster

Take a container partially filled with water. Pour slowly the plaster- of-Paris into water until water can no longer absorb any more of the powder. Seven parts of plaster to four parts water is a satisfactory mixture. The plaster is then mixed by hand until there are no lumps present, and a thick creamy consistency of mixture is obtained.

Pouring of plaster

- Pour the mixture gently into the impression. A spoon should be used to pour the mixture from a low level and to spread the plaster evenly.
- Air bubbles should be prevented. When the layer of plaster is almost one-half inch thick, place small twigs or sticks in a criss-cross pattern to reinforce the cast.
- A thin wire mesh could also be used in place of sticks.
- A second layer of plaster mixture should follow this until the cast is about one inch thick. The plaster is allowed to set for fifteen minutes.
- The setting of the cast is indicated by the rise in its temperature that can be felt by touching the cast surface.
- In order to hasten the process of hardening, one half teaspoon full of common salt may be added to the water before adding plaster, whereas, if sugar or borax is added to the mixture, the setting time gets retard.
- For identification, the cast surface should be marked with details such as the date, police station, case number, location, and signature of the investigating officer and witnesses.

Removal and cleaning

- To lift the cast, dig away the surrounding earth, remove the retaining frame gently, slip fingers under the cast, and push it slowly upwards until it is free.

- Wash the cast under a running tap or by pouring water over it to remove the adhering earth. Do not rub or scratch the surface, as that would destroy the finer details of the print.
- A clear cast will thus be obtained. Sometimes, to record finer details, a thin mixture of plaster of Paris will be required. This, however, will require a much longer setting time.

OBSERVATION

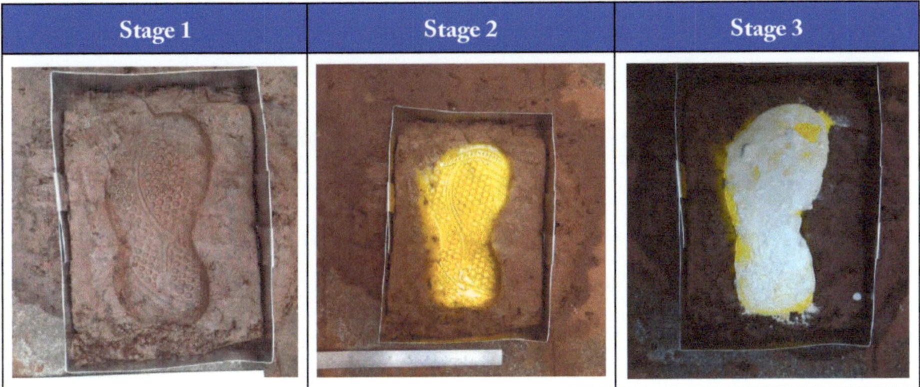

Stages of casting foot print

RESULT

The cast of footwear impression was prepared using POP or Dental stone.

FORENSIC SIGNIFICANCE

Casting is of paramount importance in forensic sciences as it allows a crime scene investigator to collect an identical copy of a mark or print from a scene, which can then be compared to a seized tool, shoe, or tire in order to establish a link between a suspect and a crime scene.

VIVA QUESTIONS

1. What is footprint casting?
2. Why is footprint casting important in forensic science?
3. What materials are used for footprint casting?
4. What is the ideal surface for footprint casting?
5. How is a footprint casting kit prepared?
6. What is the process of casting a footprint?
7. How long does it take for the casting material to set?
8. What are the different types of footprint casts?
9. How are footprint casts analyzed?
10. What are some challenges in footprint casting?
11. How are footprint casts used in crime scene investigation?
12. Can footprint casts be used in court as evidence?
13. How are footprint casts preserved?
14. Can footprint casts be used for elimination purposes?
15. What is the future of footprint casting in forensic science?

CASE STUDIES

14

GAIT PATTERN ANALYSIS

AIM

To perform the analysis of Gait pattern.

REQUIREMENTS

Gait Pattern, scale (ruler), chalk, etc.

THEORY

An individual, while walking or running, makes a series of impressions or footprints; this is called a gait pattern. A gait pattern is created due to the movement of limbs during locomotion. Gait pattern is found to be highly individualistic. Hence, it acts as evidence for solving certain crimes. Examining and analyzing the gait pattern of an individual is very important because it helps to determine the age, sex, and height of an individual. Gait normally means the manner or way in which a person walks. Since walking is an unconscious behavior, it can be used to identify an individual. Gait is an individual's biological characteristic. There are several factors that affect gait patterns, such as personality, footwear of an individual, sex, emotional behavior, speed of walking, any disorders, age, pregnancy, and light conditions. Gait patterns can be seen in most of the cases like robbery, murder, theft, housebreaking, dacoity, kidnapping, etc. Gait pattern is the most commonly encountered pattern evidence found in most crime scenes, and it helps to create a link between crime and crime. It also helps to determine the number of suspects involved in the commission of crime.

The gait pattern of an individual is analyzed as follows:

- **The direction line:** It is a straight line. It is an imaginary line drawn at the center, which helps to determine the direction of a person walking or moving.
- **The gait line:** The gait line coincides with the direction line and runs along inner sides of both heel prints, in normal person. It may vary from one individual to another because of the manner of putting down the foot. Individual who keeps their feet wide apart may create zigzag pattern. Gait line appear to be broken in pregnant women and stout persons, as they walk with feet wide apart to maintain equilibrium.
- **The foot line:** It is a straight line running through axis of the footprint longitudinally. This line passes through second toe to the center of the heel. It shows angle at which foot is put down.
- **The foot angle:** The angle between the direction line and the foot line is called as foot angle. The normal foot angle is 30-32 degrees. It varies with different individuals, and it is different for the left and right feet of the same individual. Foot angle may not change when the subject stands still, walks up and down, or carries a heavy load.
- **The principal angle:** The angle between footlines of two feet is the principal angle. And it is also the sum of foot angles. It mainly depends upon the deformities in the left or right foot.
- **The step length:** It is also called stride. It is the distance between the centers of two successive heel prints. It varies on the basis of a walker, his habits, and speed. Usually, a tall person has a longer step length than a short person. Depending on the habit, some railway workers will have longer step lengths by walking on railway tracks. The average step length of an individual varies from 20-40 inches. It can also vary with the speed of walking: 27 inches for slow walking and 35 inches for fast walking. The person running will have a maximum step length of over 40 inches.

- **The step width:** The distance between parallels drawn in the direction of direction line touching inner sides of right and left foot is step width. Step length, step width, principal angle, gait line, foot angles must be analysed and calculated to identify a possible suspect. These are unique in nature and vary from one individual to another.

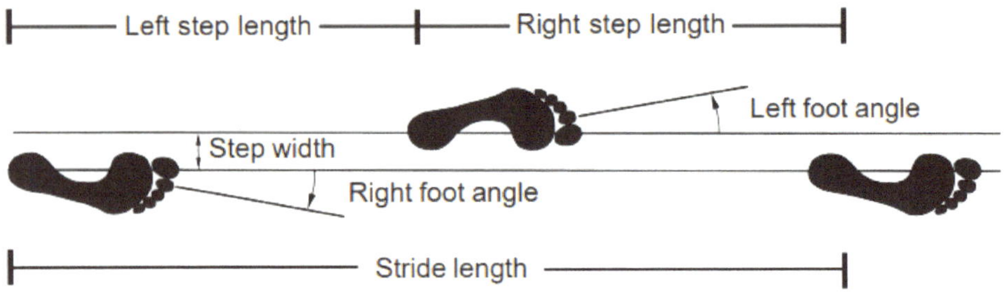

PROCEDURE

1. **Collect the Footprints:** The first step is to collect the footprints. This can be done using a variety of methods, including digital images or photographs.
2. **Analyse the Footprints:** Once the footprints have been collected, they should be analyzed. This involves looking at various features of the footprints, including the size and shape of the foot, the length and width of the stride, and the angle of the foot during each step.
3. **Identify Unique Characteristics:** The next step is to identify unique characteristics of the footprints. This may include the shape of the arch, the pattern of the toes, or the way the foot rolls during each step. These unique characteristics can be used to identify the individual who made the footprints.
4. **Compare to Known Samples:** Once unique characteristics have been identified, the footprints can be compared to known samples. This may include comparing the footprints to the footprints of known suspects or to a database of footprints from previous investigations.

5. **Make a Conclusion:** Based on the analysis and comparison of the footprints, a conclusion can be made about the identity of the individual who made the footprints. This conclusion may be used as evidence in a criminal investigation.

RESULT

The Gait pattern was successfully analyzed. Walking is something where any individual does not give much thought. As it takes place in unconscious manner, individual cannot alter his walking pattern. It is also the basic method of transportation developed by an individual and is encountered in most of the crime scene. Hence it is very important to examine and analyze gait patterns present in scene of crime.

FORENSIC SIGNIFICANCE

Gait pattern analysis is very much essential for forensic purposes because it has certain features like universality, uniqueness, and permanence.

IMPORTANCE OF ANALYSING GAIT PATTERN

Gait pattern analysis is mainly useful for personal identification. Personal identification of an individual can be done by estimating the following:

- **Age:** It is the major factor which influence walking pattern since walking depends on muscle strength. Gait pattern helps to find out whether the subject is an old or young person. Old persons drag earth by their toes while walking. Whereas young people show twisting action of toes and ball of foot. Old persons step length will be comparatively shorter. Stick marks beside the foot impressions also indicate it is old person.
- **Sex:** The sex of an individual can be determined by measuring step length. The step length of a woman tends to be lesser than that of a man. The average step length of women is 18-22 inches, and the step length of men is 25-28 inches. In a woman, the ball of the foot is narrower than that of a man. Some Indian women also wear rings on

their toes, so the bare footprint leaves the mark of rings present on their toes. This also indicates the origin of women since rings are usually worn by Indian women.

- **Height**: One cannot suggest the height of a person based on the length of the footprint, but a longer footprint and step length extending up to 30 inches suggest it to be a tall person. The short person will have a shorter step length.
- It helps in the estimation of body weight, stature, and size of the foot.
- Broken gait line suggests a subject is a sluggish person or drunkard, or it can also be a pregnant woman and persons with a load on their backs.
- Foot angle helps to differentiate an individual based on sex because men tend to have larger foot angles than women.
- Speed is also one of the major factors that alters gait patterns. The speed of the gait pattern helps to suggest whether the person is walking or running.
- The direction of movement can also be established. The pressure in the thumb and toes indicates the person was moving in the forward direction.
- The gait pattern also helps to understand the type of footwear worn and the size of footwear and also helps to determine any underlying diseases or any medical condition affecting walking patterns.
- Gait patterns also help to determine the number of possible suspects present at the crime scene.
- Features of gait help the investigator to assist in the crime investigation. It is one of the most common types of evidence left behind at the crime scene by the criminal. This provides a link between crime, criminal, and victim. It also helps in the reconstruction of the crime scene and in determining the series of events that occurred at the crime scene.
- Gait patterns may appear as imprints or sunken prints. Gait pattern usually contains soil, so soil can be collected and subjected to soil analysis; this helps in establishing the origin or location of an individual.

VIVA QUESTIONS

1. What is the purpose of gait pattern analysis in foot assessment?
2. What are the different types of foot strike patterns?
3. How does foot pronation/supination affect gait patterns?
4. What is the significance of the alignment in gait analysis?
5. How does arch height influence gait patterns?
6. What are the key events in the gait cycle?
7. How does gait pattern analysis help identify biomechanical issues?
8. What is the relationship between gait patterns and lower extremity injuries?
9. How does footwear influence gait patterns?
10. What are the differences in gait patterns between walking and running?
11. How does gait pattern analysis inform decisions on orthotics or shoe inserts?
12. What is the role of muscle strength and flexibility in gait pattern analysis?
13. How does gait pattern analysis help in assessing patients with neurological disorders?
14. What are the limitations of gait pattern analysis in foot assessment?
15. How does gait pattern analysis integrate with other assessments in foot evaluation?

CASE STUDIES

15

ANALYSIS OF PALM PRINT FOLLOWED BY ATD ANGLES OF THE SAMPLE

AIM

To analysis palm print followed by ATD angles of the sample.

THEORY

Characteristic features of palm print

The configuration of the palmar area is classifiable according to the general principles which govern the classification of fingerprints. In palm prints, the location of various features, such as proximal, ulnar, distal, and radial, are frequently used notations. The palmar surface is divisible into six topological units or configuration areas: hypothenar, thenar, and the four interdigital areas, which are formulated individually. Each configuration area of the palm is recorded as a descriptive symbol, which forms a pattern formula in this order: Hypothenar, thenar/ interdigital I, interdigital II, interdigital III, and interdigital IV. The palm area is interrupted by flexion creases, which serve as a landmark in descriptive dermatoglyphics, but they are not the components of dermatoglyphics. Flexion creases are the lines of the palm. It represents the location of the attachment of the skin to the underlying structure. These are termed white lines when viewed in prints. Major flexion creases across the palm are bracelet creases, metacarpophalangeal creases, radial longitudinal creases, distal transverse creases, and proximal transverse creases.

In palms, triradii are distinguished in terms of their location as digital triradii and axial triradii. Characteristically, there are four digital triradii located at the base of digits II, III, IV, and V in proximal relation. They are named as a, b, c, and d in radio-ulnar sequence. The four main lines originating from digital triradii are A, B, C, and D in the radio-ulnar sequence.

Main-line index

The main-line index is the sum of the two numbers corresponding to the termination of main lines A and D. The main-line formula serves as an indication of the direction of palmar ridges.

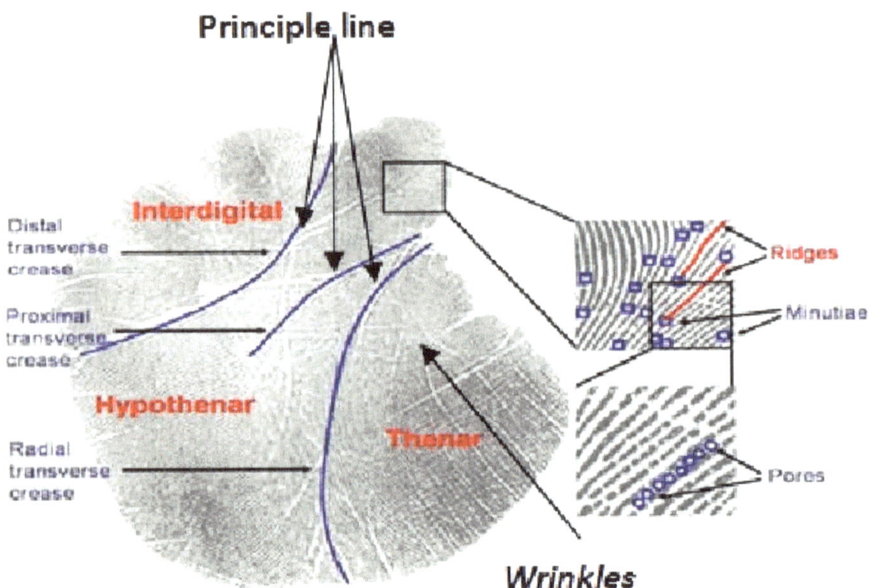

Pattern Intensity

The pattern intensity of the palm can be expressed as the sum of all triradius present.

'Atd' angle: (falls under Class characteristic)

The most widely used method for analysis of palm print is 'atd' angle. This angle is formed at the axial triradius t. The more distal the position of axial triradii tT in the palm, the larger the atd angle. atd angle is drawn from the digital triradius a to the axial triradius t, and from the axial triradius to the digital triradius d.

REQUIREMENTS

Ink pad/roller, white paper, protractor.

PROCEDURE

For atd angle measurement, the entire palm was inked, including wrist creases and hypothermal border.

1) A sheet of paper was placed on a foam rubber pad on a flat, stable surface.
2) Pressure was applied to the back of the hand to fill the concavity of the palm; otherwise, black areas would appear in the center of the palm.
3) The wrist of the person was placed on the bottom of the paper, and then the rest of the palm was pressed on the paper.
4) These palm prints were carefully observed for atd angle.
5) The atd angle formed between lines drawn from the triradii at the base of the index and little finger to the axial triradius was measured.
6) Axial triradius was designated as t and 't' or "t depending upon the proximity to the lower margin of the palm.

OBSERVATION

SAMPLE	ATD ANGLES

RESULT

The analysis of the palm print was performed, and the ATD angle of the prices was calculated.

FORENSIC SIGNIFICANCE

ATD angle, also known as the Angle of Triradius Dissociation, is a measurement used in palm print analysis. Triradii are specific ridge structures found in palm prints, and the angle formed between them, known as the ATD angle, is measured at the center of the palm. Here's how its forensic significance can be understood:

1. **Individualization**: Like fingerprints, palm prints are unique to each person.
2. **Exclusionary Evidence**: Just as a match can incriminate a suspect, the absence of a suspect's palm print at a crime scene can also be significant, potentially excluding them as a contributor to the evidence.
3. **Cold Case Resolution:** Palm prints collected from unsolved cases or crime scenes can be stored in databases for future comparison. Advances in technology and databases can lead to the identification of suspects long after the crime was committed.
4. **Evidence in Court:** Palm print evidence can be presented in court to support the prosecution's case, demonstrating the presence of a suspect at a crime scene or the handling of items of evidence.
5. **Biometric Identification**: Palm prints can also be used for non-forensic purposes such as access control systems, employee verification, and border security due to their unique nature.
6. **Statistical Analysis:** ATD angles can also be used in statistical analysis when comparing palm prints from different sources. This can be particularly useful in large-scale forensic investigations or in identifying patterns across multiple crime scenes.

In summary, palm prints hold significant forensic value in identifying individuals, corroborating evidence, linking suspects to crime scenes, and aiding in the resolution of criminal cases.

VIVA QUESTIONS

1. What is palm print analysis also known as?
2. What are the three main lines in palm print analysis?
3. What does the heart line represent?
4. What does the headline represent?
5. What does the lifeline represent?
6. What are the mounts in palm print analysis?
7. What does the Mount of Jupiter represent?
8. What does the Mount of Saturn represent?
9. How are fingerprints related to palm print analysis?
10. What is the significance of palm shape in analysis?
11. How does palm print analysis relate to psychology?
12. Can palm print analysis predict the future?
13. How is palm print analysis used in forensic science?
14. What is the difference between palm print analysis and handwriting analysis?
15. How does palm print analysis vary across cultures?

CASE STUDIES

16

TO STUDY HIERARCHY AND DIFFERENT DIVISIONS OF FORENSIC SCIENCE LABORATORY

AIM

To study Hierarchy and different divisions of Forensic science Laboratory.

REQUIREMENTS

Research paper, online data, online articles etc.

THEORY

HIERARCHY OF FSL

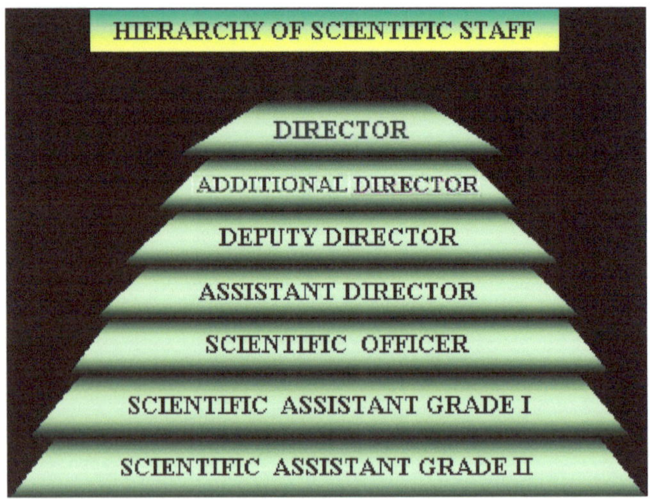

DIVISIONS IN FSL

Chemistry and Explosives

The minimum qualification of the reporting officer in chemistry should be a Graduate in Science with chemistry as one of the subjects or equivalent from a recognised university with at least five years' experience in a relevant field or postgraduate in chemistry / specialization in relevant field or equivalent from a recognised university with at least two years' experience in relevant field.

Toxicology

The minimum qualification for the reporting officer shall be a Graduate in Science with chemistry/biochemistry as one of the subjects or equivalent from a recognised university with at least five years' experience in a relevant field or postgraduate in chemistry/biochemistry/specialization in relevant field or equivalent from a recognised university with at least two years experience in relevant field. Toxicologists must be competent in performing qualitative analyses of drugs, metabolites, and other toxic substances in biological materials. They must also be able to make a systematic search for such substances and apply appropriate extractive and separator procedures.

Biology and Serology

The minimum qualification for the reporting officer shall be a Graduate in Science with biology as one of the subjects or equivalent from a recognised university with at least five years' experience in a relevant field or postgraduate in any biological science/specialization in a relevant field or equivalent from a recognised university with at least two years experience in relevant field. Serologists must have a knowledge of basic biological sciences and sufficient knowledge of chemistry to understand the procedures used. They must also have adequate knowledge of the statistics used in forensic serology.

DNA Finger Printing

The minimum qualification for the reporting officer shall be a Graduate in biological science / forensic science with genetics as one of the subjects or equivalent from a recognised university with at least five years' experience in a relevant field or a postgraduate in biological science / forensic science/ specialization in genetics or relevant field or equivalent from a recognised university with at least two years experience in relevant field. He/she must have knowledge of scientific literature, procedures/protocols, and practices relevant to DNA testing. They must have the necessary skills to evaluate and interpret the results of those tests. They must also have an adequate knowledge of population genetics and the statistics used in forensic DNA examinations.

Physics

The minimum qualification of the reporting officer in physics should be a Graduate in Science with physics as one of the subjects or equivalent from the recognised university with at least five years' experience in a relevant field or postgraduate in physics/specialization in a relevant field or equivalent from a recognised university with at least two years experience in relevant field.

Ballistics

The minimum qualification for the reporting officer shall be a Graduate in Science with physics as one of the subjects or equivalent from a recognised university with at least five years' experience in a relevant field or a postgraduate in physics/specialization in a relevant field or equivalent from a recognised university with at least two years experience in relevant field. Ballistic Experts should have sufficient knowledge of microscopy, superior lighting methods, preparation of impressions or casts, methods of relative investigation, and the conception of individualization. They must also have adequate knowledge of the nomenclature and operation of firearms, bullet and cartridge case comparisons, powder and shot patterns, distance determinations, and types of firearm determination from a discharged cartridge case or bullet.

Questioned Documents

The essential requirement of the reporting officer in the questioned document should be a Bachelors in Science with physics/chemistry/forensic science as one of the subjects or comparable from a recognised university with a minimum of five years experience in a relevant field or postgraduate in physics/chemistry/specialization in relevant field or equivalent from a recognised university with at least two years experience in relevant field. Questioned Document Experts should possess an awareness of the main beliefs of photography, microscopy, relative analysis, and individualization. They must also have satisfactory knowledge of writing or printing instruments/processes, as well as ink, paper, and copying processes.

Forensic Psychology

The minimum qualification for the reporting officer shall be a postgraduate in psychology / specialization in a relevant field or equivalent from a recognised university with at least two years of experience in the relevant field.

Fingerprints

The minimum qualification for the reporting officer shall be a Graduate in Science from a recognised university with at least five years' experience in a relevant field or a postgraduate in science with a specialization in a relevant field or equivalent from a recognised university with at least two years experience in relevant field. They must have adequate knowledge of comparative examination techniques and methods of processing, recovering, and presenting latent prints.

Crime Scene Investigation

The minimum qualification for the reporting officer shall be a Graduate in Science from a recognised university with at least five years' experience in a relevant field or a postgraduate in science with a specialization in a relevant field or equivalent from a recognised university with at least two years experience in relevant field. Crime Scene investigators should possess extensive experience and be trained in the discipline. They must be competent in the application of principles of crime scene photography, scene examination, exhibit handling, and their safety, and they must have adequate knowledge of other disciplines. They should be competent to independently perform the assessment of the crime scene. In addition, every reporting officer must have a good understanding of the principles, uses, and limitations of the instruments and the methods and procedures applied to the tasks performed.

RESULT

The Hierarchy and Divisions of FSL have been studied successfully.

VIVA QUESTIONS

1. What is the main goal of a forensic science laboratory?
2. What is the typical hierarchy of a forensic science laboratory?
3. What are the main divisions of a forensic science laboratory?
4. Which division processes DNA evidence?
5. Which division analyses drugs and poisons?
6. Which division examines evidence from crime scenes?
7. Which division analyzes firearms and tool marks?
8. Which division recovers and analyzes digital evidence?
9. What is the role of a forensic scientist in the laboratory?
10. What is the role of a technician in the laboratory?
11. How many sections are typically in a crime lab?
12. What is the importance of quality control in a forensic laboratory?
13. What is the role of a director in a forensic laboratory?
14. How do forensic laboratories ensure a chain of custody?
15. What is the significance of accreditation in a forensic laboratory?

CASE STUDIES

SOURCES AND REFERENCES

1. https://slideplayer.com/slide/10694260/#google_vignette
2. https://ebrary.net/161552/law/ridge_tracing_counting_whorl_patterns
3. https://encryptedtbn0.gstatic.com/images?q=tbn:ANd9GcRESmfb-BNsJTopnJMTBbQfF2a9I5VIAX42pzA&s
4. https://www.researchgate.net/publication/310953935/figure/fig2/AS:667722568437763@1536208874213/palm-print-image-Principle-line-ridges-and-valleys-of-palm30-Table-I-Type-of.png
5. What Is a Fingerprint? Definition, Types, Trends (2024). 31/12/2022. https://www.aratek.co/news/what-is-a-fingerprint
6. https://forensicreader.com/henry-fingerprint-classification-system/
7. https://www.coursehero.com/tutors-problems/Biology/52953854-Identify-the-fingerprint-Tented-arch-Central-pocket/
8. https://pslc.ws/macrog/kidsmac/firehouse/arson/fbiprint.htm
9. https://slideplayer.com/slide/17082818/
10. https://forensicreader.com/primary-classification-of-fingerprint/
11. https://i.ytimg.com/vi/L-biU2Xfdtg/hq720.jpg?sqp=-

BIOGRAPHY OF DR. RAJU NANDHAKUMAR

Dr. R. Nandhakumar specialises in organic and supramolecular chemistry. He received both his UG, PG, and Ph.D. degrees in Chemistry from Bharathiar University, Coimbatore, Tamil Nadu, India. Presently, he is the Professor of Chemistry at the Division of Physical Sciences, Karunya Institute of Technology and Science. His research interests include bio-organic chemistry, carbon-based materials, fluorescent chemosensors, and chirality and forensic sciences. He has successfully completed several projects from various funding agencies and guided six doctoral students. To his credit, he has written four books, seven book chapters, two international patents (granted), fifteen national patents (twelve granted), and published more than 190 research papers (including five review articles) in peer-reviewed international and national journals. He is also the director of the company Four I R & D Tech Solutions, PVT Ltd., Coimbatore, which is a startup company.

BIOGRAPHY OF MS. LABHINI RAHANGDALE

Miss. Labhini Rahangdale holds a Master of Science degree in Forensic Science and is currently an Assistant Professor specializing in forensic fingerprint and questioned document analysis. With two years of teaching experience, Miss. Labhini Rahangdale has effectively imparted knowledge in various forensic subjects, ensuring that students gain a comprehensive understanding of the field. Miss. Labhini Rahangdale has also qualified for the University Grants Commission National Eligibility Test (UGC NET). Before transitioning to academia, Miss. Labhini Rahangdale served as a senior forensic analyst for a private company. In this role, Miss. Labhini Rahangdale was responsible for handling a variety of fire and arson-related cases, applying rigorous scientific methods and critical thinking to solve complex forensic challenges. Miss. Labhini Rahangdale's knowledge of fingerprint and questioned document analysis, combined with practical experience in the field, makes her a valuable contributor to both the academic and professional forensic communities.

www.ingramcontent.com/pod-product-compliance
Ingram Content Group UK Ltd.
Pitfield, Milton Keynes, MK11 3LW, UK
UKHW061027310726
14090UKWH00024B/440

* 9 7 9 8 8 9 5 4 4 0 7 0 4 *